THE HAND OF THE LORD

Society of Biblical Literature

The Hand of the Lord
by Patrick D. Miller Jr. and J. J. M. Roberts

THE HAND OF THE LORD
A Reassessment of the "Ark Narrative" of 1 Samuel

Patrick D. Miller Jr.
J. J. M. Roberts

Society of Biblical Literature
Atlanta

THE HAND OF THE LORD

Library of Congress Cataloging-in-Publication Data

Miller, Patrick D.
The hand of the Lord: a reassessment of the "Ark narrative" of 1 Samuel / Patrick D. Miller, Jr., J. J. M. Roberts.
p. cm.
Originally published: Baltimore : Johns Hopkins University Press, c1977, in series: Johns Hopkins University. Near Eastern Studies.
Includes bibliographical references and indexes.
ISBN 978-1-58983-294-7 (paper binding : alk. paper)
1. Bible. O.T. Samuel, 1st, II, 12–VII, 1—Theology. 2. Ark of the Covenant. I. Roberts, J. J. M. (Jimmy Jack McBee), 1939- II. Title.
BS1325.52.M55 2008
222'.4306—dc22 2007036001

16 15 14 13 12 11 10 09 08 5 4 3 2 1
Printed in the United States of America on acid-free, recycled paper conforming to ANSI/NISO Z39.48-1992 (R1997) and ISO 9706:1994 standards for paper permanence.

CONTENTS

Preface vii

Abbreviations viii

1. Introduction to the Study 1

2. The Extent of the Narrative 27

3. Exegesis of 1 Samuel 2:12–17, 22–25, 27–36 37

4. Exegesis of 1 Samuel 4 43

5. Exegesis of 1 Samuel 5 53

6. Exegesis of 1 Samuel 6 69

7. The Structure and Intention of 1 Samuel 2:12–17, 22–25, 27–36; 4:1b–7:1 79

Appendix 95

Bibliography 107

Index 113

PREFACE

This book had its inception out of the coincidence that both authors independently and within a short period presented papers on aspects of the so-called "Ark Narrative" to The Colloquium for Old Testament Research (Miller) and The Biblical Colloquium (Roberts). Each of us had an opportunity to hear or read the other's paper. The discovery that we had pursued different aspects of the passage within a common understanding of its nature and purpose that did not generally correspond to the scholarly consensus about these chapters led us to combine efforts in a larger study of this important unit that would give due attention to the illumination of it by reference to comparative materials, to the careful exegesis of its component parts, and to an overall analysis of its theological character.

The work presented here is a joint effort in the full sense of the term. While each author necessarily had to prepare basic drafts of parts of the book, both authors participated fully in the shaping and content of all parts. The accomplishment of such a cooperative literary and scholarly endeavor has turned out to be more feasible and enjoyable than we had expected and encourages us about the possibility and usefulness of such team projects.

We would like to express our gratitude to The Johns Hopkins University Press and the editors of the The Johns Hopkins Near Eastern Studies for including this volume in that distinguished series.

ABBREVIATIONS

The abbreviations used in this work follow the style sheet of the Journal of Biblical Literature. Biblical works not listed in that work are cited according to the index of abbreviations given in Otto Eissfeldt's standard *The Old Testament: An Introduction* (trans. P. R. Ackroyd; New York: Harper & Row, 1965), 854–61. Assyriological works are cited according to the *Chicago Assyrian Dictionary* or R. Borger's *Handbuch der Keilschriftliteratur* (3 vols.; Berlin: de Gruyter, 1967–1875).

1
INTRODUCTION TO THE STUDY

In light of the two monographs on the ark narratives of 1 Samuel recently published by Franz Schicklberger[1] and Antony Campbell,[2] one may well question the need for a new monograph on the same topic. Certainly their work has rendered some aspects of the typical monograph redundant in this case. Schicklberger's summary[3] and especially Campbell's survey[4] of the earlier investigation of the ark narratives are adequate and need not be repeated as an introduction to our own analysis of the narratives. Even on the more detailed level, Schicklberger's critique[5] of Leonhard Rost's basic study[6] is cogent enough that one need not rehash Rost's views before proceeding to an explication of one's own. Moreover, one must commend both Schicklberger and Campbell for following up a potentially fruitful insight of M. Delcor.[7] They again call attention to the extrabiblical texts concerning the capture and return of divine images[8] that Delcor had noted as providing possible parallels to the biblical ark narratives.[9] This openness to the broader cultural context in which Israel's faith developed could freshen up a scholarly discussion grown stale within the narrow confines

1. *Die Ladeerzählungen des ersten Samuel-Buches, Eine literaturwissenschaftliche und theologiegeschichtliche Untersuchung* (Forschung zur Bibel 7; Würzburg: Echter, 1973).

2. *The Ark Narrative (1 Sam 4–6; 2 Sam 6): A Form-Critical and Traditio-Historical Study* (SBLDS 16; Missoula, Mont.: SBL and Scholars' Press, 1975).

3. *Ladeerzählungen*, 11–12, 17–25.

4. *Ark Narrative*, 1-54.

5. *Ladeerzählungen*, 11–17.

6. Leonhard Rost, *Die Überlieferung von der Thronnachfolge* Davids (BWANT 111/6; Stuttgart: Kohlhammer, 1926); reprinted in Rost's *Das kleine Credo und andere Studien zum Alten Testament* (Heidelberg: Quelle & Meyer, 1965), 119–253.

7. M. Delcor, "Jahweh et Dagon ou le Jahwisme face à la religion des Philistins, d'après 1 Sam. V," *VT* 14 (1964): 136–54.

8. Schicklberger, *Ladeerzählungen*, 149, 181–86; Campbell, *Ark Narrative*, 179–91.

9. *VT* 14 (1964), 138.

of internal biblical analysis. Scholarly discussion of the ark narrative has undoubtedly suffered from a strange lack of interest in extrabiblical parallels[10]—a point to which we must return.

Nevertheless, while Schicklberger and Campbell have made our work easier, they have not made it unnecessary. We cannot accept the radically different literary-critical analysis of either author, and given that basic disagreement, it is not surprising that we must also reject much of their form- and genre-critical analyses, as well as their views on the date and intention of the narrative. Moreover, neither Schicklberger nor Campbell, as refreshing as their use of the comparative material is, exploits fully the valuable insights these sources provide.

Schicklberger

Schicklberger's analytic work is quite original and will require a detailed discussion.

The *Katastrophenerzählung*

The key element in Schicklberger's interpretation is his isolation and interpretation of 1 Sam 4:1a(LXX)b, 2–4, 10–12, 13 (without *whnh ʿly yšb ʿl hksʾ),* 14b–18a, 19–21 as an old, relatively complete, "novelistic catastrophe narrative."[11] He bases this analysis first of all on literary-critical observations that suggest the separation of 1 Sam 4 from the following

10. Hugo Gressmann is one of the very few commentators of any note, prior to Delcor, who cites parallels (*Die älteste Geschichtsschreibung und Prophetie Israels* [SAT 2/1; Göttingen: Vandenhoeck & Ruprecht, 1921], 16), and they are all quite late, if not remote. Most scholars after Gressmann seem to have given up the search for comparative material. Leonard Rost's treatment of the ark narrative—the only one ever to achieve even a limited consensus—totally ignores the question of literary parallels, and few of his later critics have improved on him in this regard. Even such thoroughgoing myth-and-ritual partisans as Sigmund Mowinckel (*The Psalms in Israel's Worship* [2 vols.; New York: Abingdon, 1962], 1:175–76) and Aage Bentzen ("The Cultic Use of the Story of the Ark in Samuel," *JBL* 67 [1948]: 37–53) have been content with quite general comparisons between 2 Sam 6 and the cultic rites and processions associated with the Babylonian New Year festival. Even less understandable is the lack of interest recent commentators have shown in Delcor's parallels. Hans Joachim Stoebe, for instance, cites Delcor's work and then proceeds to ignore it in his exegesis of 1 Sam 5–6 (*Das erste Buch Samuelis* [KAT 8/1; Gütersloh: Mohn, 1973], 138ff.).

11. *Ladeerzählungen*, 42, 70, 177.

chapters. Schicklberger repeats the old argument that the theology of the ark reflected in 1 Sam 4 is basically different from that found in the other sections attributed to the ark narrative.[12] In addition, he points to certain features of Rost's word statistics that, in Schicklberger's view, imply an originally separate existence for chapter 1 Sam 4.[13]

However, 1 Sam 4 cannot be removed in a piece, for, as Schicklberger correctly observes, the literary ties between 1 Sam 4:5–9 and 1 Sam 5–6 are too intimate to be secondary.[14] Schicklberger himself, while noting the literary connection between 1 Sam 4:5–9 and 1 Sam 5–6, does not cite this as an argument for excising 4:5–9 from 1 Sam 4—this observation, if made too soon, would weaken his case for the independence of chapter 4—but the evidence he does cite for removing verses 5–9 is so weak that one may suspect this insight as the real, hidden motivation for such surgery. As his putative reasons, Schicklberger points to a slowing down of the action with the *wyhy* of verse 5,[15] a loss of interest in the continuation of the events,[16] and a shift of emphasis from the battle to the ark.[17] He concludes with the syntactical argument, "Had verse 10 been attached to verse 9 originally, *plštym* would have been superfluous as the subject of *wylḥnw*."[18] None of these arguments is in the least compelling. The slowdown in the action begins not in verse 5 but in verse 4, with the introduction of the two sons of Eli, Hophni and Phinehas. Schicklberger's next two reasons are extremely subjective and reflect a rather wooden, mechanical criticism that mistakes every little shift in a narrator's attention for a new source. His syntactical point cannot be taken seriously. One could omit *plštym*, but given the mention of *'brym* after the last occurrence of *plštym* in verse 9, the repetition of *plštym* in verse 10 adds clarity and can hardly be considered a striking redundancy.

If his literary-critical analysis is less than convincing, Schicklberger's form-critical analysis is even weaker. According to him, 1 Sam 4:1a(LXX)b, 2–4, 10–12, 13 (without *whnh 'ly yšb 'l hks'*), 14b–18a, 19–21 originated as an oral narrative about a historical Israelite defeat soon after the cata-

12. Ibid., 13.
13. Ibid.
14. Ibid., 86–99.
15. Ibid., 29.
16. Ibid.
17. Ibid., 30.
18. Ibid., 31.

strophic events it relates had occurred.[19] The author of this narrative came from the Ephraimite circles most directly affected by these events, perhaps even from Shilo itself.[20] Who else, Schicklberger asks, could have known all the details about the ark, the route of the messenger, and the fate of the various Elides?[21] Moreover, the audience to which this author first addressed his narrative must probably be sought among the Shilonites or people within Shilo's immediate vicinity, for otherwise one would expect a more detailed introduction of Eli and his sons.[22] But what motivated this author to compose such a narrative? Schicklberger's answer to this crucial question is so bizarre that it deserves to be quoted in full:

> What can have induced the narrator and the tradents to speak of the unfortunate course of the battle and the shocking events. Doubtless simply the endeavor to make known and to hand down what totally unheard of, unprecedented event occurred "at that time." They narrated what and how it had occurred. In so doing they felt their way forward into theological virgin territory. Out of the experience of the political adversity and the military debacle the freedom of Yahweh in history is recognized; he remains the free lord of his decisions and does not owe Israel the victory.[23]

Such an analysis would be far more convincing if Schicklberger could cite another ancient Near Eastern example of his *Katastrophenerzählung* genre. In the absence of parallels, one can hardly ignore the nagging presence of numerous unanswered and disturbing questions. If the narrative was early and addressed to a Shilonite audience familiar with the Elides, why was it necessary at all? Surely not for mere information. The details of so shocking a defeat, suffered at one's doorsteps within the relatively recent past, must have been too deeply etched on everyone's memory to require any reminder of merely "what had happened." This must have been common knowledge, painful to recall, and any narrative with no more point than to recite the details of this national disgrace would hardly be well received if it is conceivable at all. One could understand an attempt to explain why such a disaster occurred—Israelite and other Near Eastern

19. Ibid., 70–72.
20. Ibid., 72.
21. Ibid.
22. Ibid., 73.
23. Ibid.

literature is full of interpretive narratives about national catastrophes—but Schicklberger explicitly denies that his author had any such didactic purpose,[24] and given his literary analysis, there is no trace of an explanation. None of the questions his truncated narrative raises are answered. Why did the Israelites lose the battle? Was Yahweh overpowered by the Philistines? If not, why did he permit them to capture his ark and kill his priests? In fact, even the minimal theology Schicklberger tries to sneak into his narrative is absent from the account as it stands in his analysis. In isolation, 1 Sam 4:1a(LXX)b, 2–4, 10–12, 13, 14b–18a, 19–21, far from suggesting Yahweh's freedom in history, points rather to his defeat. Schicklberger sees this clearly for 4:5–9,[25] but his attempt to avoid the same embarrassment for his expurgated *Katastrophenerzählung* is unsuccessful.[26] The ark may not be as central or as intimately tied to Yahweh in his narrative as it is in verses 5–9, but it is still central and intimate enough to suggest defeat rather than freedom, and the attention given the fate of the Elides only strengthens this impression. By Schicklberger's analysis the narrative treats each of the Elides positively, as faithful priests,[27] and the unexplained, unrequited death of men so near to God hardly argues for Yahweh's freedom. Neither the Deuteronomistic Historian nor the Chronicler could simply relate the death of a figure like Josiah, and one may doubt whether Schicklberger's earlier narrator could treat a similarly disillusioning event with greater, unparalleled equanimity.

---

24. Ibid., 70–71.

25. Ibid., 86–87: "Thus it would have been impossible for Israelite sensibility and would speak against every rule of narrative art to take up a narrative section that underscored the self-assurance and the *obdurateness of the Philistines* against Yahweh to such an extent (cf. v. 9), in a context that ended with 4:21, therefore, for all practical purposes, in an endorsement of the Philistines and the capture of the ark, which had been portrayed as fear-inspiring. That would have implied that the Philistines had successfully resisted Yahweh and remained superior to him."

26. Ibid., 87 n. 193: "In contrast, the old catastrophe narrative can very well conclude with the mention of the loss of the ark, since in it the ark does not stand so much in the center of the narrative as in verses 5ff. The fate of the Elides is paid no less attention than the ark. Moreover, the ark is not sketched in so narrow a relationship to Yahweh as is the case in 4:5ff, so its capture by the Philistines does not also imply a defeat of Yahweh."

27. Ibid., 15, 36, 62.

The Later Narrative

Having rejected Schicklberger's analysis of what he takes to be the kernel around which the later development of the ark narratives crystallized, one could hardly expect us to accept his analysis of this supposedly later material. It may be helpful to review Schicklberger's treatment, nevertheless, especially with regard to dating and theological intent.

He isolates 1 Sam 4:5–9; 5:1–6bα, 7–12; 6:1–4*, 5aβ–11abα, 12–14, 16 as a new treatment of the events connected with the loss of the ark, a treatment that is totally independent of the narrative about David's transfer of the ark in 2 Sam 6 but dependent on and incorporating the earlier *Katastrophenerzählung*.[28] The introduction of this new material shifts the emphasis of the narrative in chapter 4 away from Israel's defeat and the fate of the Elides and centers it on the ark of God and its confrontation with the Philistines.[29] In doing so, the restructured narrative betrays a new intellectual concern for the close tie between Yahweh and his ark and raises the expectation of a display of God's power against the Philistines.[30] This second account, then, is no mere recounting of what had happened. Its author was not interested in mere history; he was a theologian, and Schicklberger designates his work a "composed theological narrative tale."[31]

While the *Katastrophenerzählung* appears to have been composed in Israel and reflects northern interests, Schicklberger places the author of this more reflective account in Jerusalem.[32] Since it is dependent on the earlier narrative, however, he raises the question of when such northern traditions might have come to Jerusalem. For Schicklberger the obvious answer is after the fall of Samaria, around 720 B.C.[33]

Other indices also suggest that the composition of this later work took place in the late eighth or early seventh century, during the reign of Hezekiah.[34] Yahweh's defeat of the Philistines, unaided by humans, reflects a late stage in the development of holy-war ideology closely associated with

28. Ibid., 170ff.

29. Ibid., 180.

30. Ibid.

31. The German is "komponierte theologische Aussageerzählung" (ibid., 175).

32. Ibid., 180.

33. Ibid.

34. Ibid., 230, 233–34.

Isaiah's theology.[35] Moreover, God's heavy dependence on the weapon of plague in the expanded narrative suggests Yahweh had by this time taken over the role of Reshep and probably reflects a polemic against the renewed importance of this Canaanite plague god brought about by the introduction of his Mesopotamian analogue Nergal after 722 B.C.[36] The etiology about skipping over the door sill may also point to this general period, since such a practice appears to have been introduced into Israel as a specifically Assyrian custom sometime in the eighth or early seventh century, being attested by Zephaniah somewhat later in the seventh century B.C.[37] Moreover, the closest parallels to the sacrifice in 1 Sam 6:14 are to be found in Gideon's action in Judg 6:26 and Elijah's in 1 Kgs 18.[38] Both of these texts date from the period after Jehu's revolt[39] and may, therefore, have provided the model for our author's later polemic against pagan gods.

The central concern in this "composed theological narrative," however, is not a polemic against pagan gods. There is perhaps a political polemic against the Philistines because of border disputes stemming from the conflicts in Hezekiah's time,[40] but even that is not the main thrust of the narrative. Schicklberger's theologian was primarily concerned to counteract the growing importance of the "modern" Zion theology.[41] He wanted to restore the ark to theological significance.[42] His narrative's interest is

> to prove and to make vivid that the ark (afterward as before) is the place of Yahweh's presence. The old conception of the ark which had been taken up in the Zion tradition is revived (due to the initiative of fugitive North Israelites) as the central theme of a theological treatise.[43]

Our response to this thesis can be kept brief, since the explication of our own views in the chapters to follow will make it quite clear where and why we disagree with Schicklberger. There are many weaknesses in his

35. Ibid., 187.
36. Ibid., 196–97.
37. Ibid., 199–200.
38. Ibid., 205–6.
39. Ibid.
40. Ibid., 230, 231–34.
41. Ibid., 224.
42. Ibid., 225.
43. Ibid., 236.

reconstruction, but perhaps the most glaring is his failure to explain the continued interest of north Israelites in ark theology when the object of their concern had been lost to them since the split under Rehoboam. Even if one could believe in the existence of Schicklberger's early *Katastrophenerzählung*, it is difficult to see why it would be handed down for over two hundred years or, giving its seeming indifference to the loss of the ark, how it could become a central document in a north Israelite group consumed by ark piety.

Schicklberger's positive arguments for dating are certainly not strong enough to overcome this obvious problem. The narrative's nonsynergistic portrayal of Yahweh's victory over the Philistines need not be attributed to the later development of holy-war ideology; it could just as easily spring from the historical memory that Israel had nothing to do with the return of the ark. The polemic against pagan plague gods is too subtle to base anything on its assumed existence, and were it demonstrable, that would still be no reason to date the text to the late eighth or early seventh century. Both Reshep and Nergal were known in Palestine from the second millennium,[44] and, as far as we know, faithful Yahwists had always regarded Yahweh as the cause of disease, indeed of every good or evil.[45] The parallel between the sacrifice of the men of Beth-shemesh and that of Gideon or Elijah is not convincing, but even if it were, and one accepted Schicklberger's dating of these two stories of Gideon and Elijah, one could still argue for the reverse order of dependency, that is, the ark narrative could be the

44. Reshep was certainly known. He is well attested at Ugarit, Cyprus, and Egypt from the last half of the second millennium (M. J. Dahood, "Ancient Semitic Deities in Syria and Palestine," in *Le antiche divinità Semitiche* [Studi Semitici 1; Rome: Centro di studi semitici, Istituto di studi orientali, Università, 1958], 83–85). While the evidence for Nergal is less abundant, he does occur at Ugarit (E. von Weiher, *Der babylonische Gott Nergal* [AOAT 11; Neukirchen-Vluyn: Neukirchener, 1971], 90–91), and a fragment of the myth of Nergal and Erishkigal was discovered in the El Amarna archive (J. A. Knudtzon, *Die El-Amarna-Tafeln* [VAB 2; Leipzig: Hinrichs, 1915], no. 357).

45. The narrow compartmentalization of divine functions that Schicklberger's discussion assumes cannot be supported textually for Yahweh, and it does not ring true, even for the gods of Israel's polytheistic neighbors. Other gods besides plague gods sometimes get credit for decimating the population with disease. In stressing Yahweh's assumption of the plague god's role, Schicklberger refers at length *(Ladeerzählungen,* 189–90) to Roberts's earlier study of the expression "hand of the god X ("The Hand of Yahweh," *VT* 21 [1971]: 244–51), but this expression, which refers to divinely imposed illness, occurs with about forty different divine names (ibid., 256), and most of them are by no means plague gods.

earliest of the three. Finally, the practice of skipping over the door sill is too pervasive an apotropaic rite to date anything on its appearance in a narrative,[46] particularly when the etiology itself may be secondary.[47]

Campbell

Campbell's literary-critical analysis will require less discussion. He basically follows Rost in analyzing 1 Sam 4:1b–7:1; 2 Sam 6:2–23 as a complete, self-contained, independent narrative.[48] He differs from Rost by including 1 Sam 4:22; 6:5–9, 17–18; and 2 Sam 6:16, 20–23 as original parts of the narrative.[49] Only 1 Sam 4:18b and 6:15 must be excised as secondary additions.[50] Since our judgments on these matters have been hinted at in the discussion of Schicklberger's work and will be dealt with in detail in our exegetical treatment, we may pass on to some brief remarks on Campbell's view of the intention of the narrative.

According to Campbell, the theological intent of the narrative is to designate the end of the old epoch in Israel's history as Yahweh's doing and to indicate that Yahweh looks with favor on the new political epoch, that is, the Davidic era in Jerusalem.[51] At the same time, the insistence on Yahweh's freedom qualifies this legitimation of the new political situation. As Campbell says,

> It is not a simple acceptance of a political status quo, which is given the blessing of the Lord after the fact. To the contrary, it expresses a marked distance from the political powers. Not only was a previous political situation rejected (1 Sam 4), but the statement of the acceptance of the new is clearly conditioned by the will of Yahweh. At Perez-uzzah, the king was put on notice.[52]

---

46. See the discussion and additional sources cited by Herbert Donner, "Die Schwellenhüpfer: Beobachtungen zu Zephanja 1,8f.," *JSS* 15 (1970): 53. Unlike Zeph 1:9, 1 Sam 5:5 says nothing about such a practice being current in Israel. The situation reflected in the two verses is not the same, and there is no reason why these two references must be dated to the same period. They could be separated by hundreds of years.

47. See below, chapter 5.

48. *Ark Narrative*, 165–78.

49. Ibid., 166–68.

50. Ibid., 168.

51. Ibid., 201.

52. Ibid., 202.

While it is the beginning of the narrative that tells of the end of the epoch and the end of the narrative that legitimizes the new, it is the middle that stresses Yahweh's freedom and initiative in the matter.[53] Though it depicts the sovereign movement of Yahweh as a second exodus, it is not an exodus that automatically leads to Israel. Yahweh's leisurely sojourn in Philistia, his lengthy stay in the Israelite boondocks, and the dangerous potential manifested in the Perez-uzzah incident all tend to "evoke the possibility that Yahweh might not have chosen to renew his relationship with his people."[54] Campbell suggests that this may even be the reason why Samuel and Saul are completely ignored by the narrative:

> Could it be that from the standpoint of the narrator, they belonged to a period when Yahweh stood aloof from Israel, and that such a period could be treated as if it had never been. More exactly expressed, such a period could not be concerned with the military and political machinations of men; such a period could only be concerned with anxiously waiting for Yahweh.[55]

Campbell's theological interpretation is dependent, of course, on his analysis of where the ark narrative begins and ends, and since we differ at this point, our view of the intention of the narrative will also differ. This more basic question of the extent of the narrative will be taken up in the next chapter, but even here some preliminary comments on Campbell's theological interpretation are in order.

In the first place, it is difficult to reconcile his totally unexplained end of an epoch with certain features of the narrative as he delimits it. He insists that

> there is no discussion or consideration of the cause of this end. It is not attributed to any sin, any national fault, any breach of covenant.... No cause is alleged. It is not an end, "because"—it is simply an end.[56]

But such an analysis does not do justice to the important question raised by the Israelites in 1 Sam 4:3, "Why has Yahweh defeated us today before the Philistines?" Though he sees the importance of the question for the

53. Ibid., 204–5.
54. Ibid., 206.
55. Ibid., 206–7.
56. Ibid., 200.

intention of the author,[57] on Campbell's analysis that question is never answered.[58] The continuation of the narrative merely underlines the fact that it was indeed Yahweh who defeated Israel,[59] but it never explains why. To say that Yahweh defeated Israel because he rejected the old epoch does not answer the question; it simply rephrases it with an even more insistent "Why?" Any analysis that leaves unanswered this key question, explicitly raised by the narrative itself, must be suspect. Moreover, one should note that none of the related material in which Campbell finds a similar periodization of history leaves the reason for Yahweh's rejection of his people similarly hidden in God's own arbitrary nature.[60] Yahweh's actions were not arbitrary, but a righteous response to the people's sins. The uniqueness of the ark narrative in this respect should raise doubts about the validity of Campbell's analysis.

One other point should be noted before passing on to the comparative material. Campbell's overall understanding of the narrative causes him to read into the material an excessive emphasis on Yahweh's freedom. The following remark is quite instructive in this regard:

> Of itself, the divination simply determines the answer to the question of v. 9, as to where the responsibility for the trouble lies. But in the context of the overall narrative, it puts the responsibility for the return of the ark (with all that this implies) where alone it belongs—in the freedom of Yahweh's choice.[61]

According to Campbell, therefore, the basic function of the divination episode within the narrative structure is to give the initiative in the return to Yahweh alone.[62]

In our opinion, this comes perilously close to eisegesis. A more sober exegesis must pay more attention to his exegetical observation that "the divination simply determines the answer to the question of v. 9." Whether "simply" is an appropriate word in this sentence, however, may be questioned. There is certainly a deeper level in this material than the surface

57. Ibid., 64–65.
58. Ibid., 92.
59. Ibid., 156.
60. Ibid., 211–39.
61. Ibid., 161.
62. Ibid.

structure of the narrative as story,[63] but one cannot find that deeper level by skipping too quickly from the actual wording of the text to "the context of the overall narrative." The Philistines want to know whether it was really Yahweh who was responsible for their discomfiture, and the divination functions on the surface to answer that question. Why, though, was it important for the narrator to have the Philistines raise the question? Whose question was he really answering in recounting the results of the divination? The deeper theological structure of the narrative can only be grasped by pursuing this question actually raised in the text; to stress the idea of Yahweh's freedom at this point is to divert attention away from the text and can only lead to a misunderstanding of its theological intent.

Comparative Material

Schicklberger's citation of extrabiblical sources about the capture and return of divine images,[64] if not dependent upon, is at least anticipated by Delcor's observation that the ark narrative treats the ark as the functional equivalent of a divine image among Israel's neighbors.[65] Schicklberger has performed a service in recalling this largely ignored insight to scholarly attention, but despite a number of good observations, he fails to exploit this insight fully. He is satisfied with a mere description of the treatment accorded captured images. After quoting a few representative texts, he passes on to other concerns without ever trying to get behind the actions to the ideology that motivated such treatment of the images.

Campbell, on the other hand, is correctly concerned with the ideology behind such action, but he ignores some of the most interesting parallels,[66] and, in our opinion, he does not take the theological problem raised by the capture of one's gods seriously enough. His treatment suggests that the official theology of the defeated was easily accepted by the defeated people—that such disasters did not raise doubts in anyone's mind about the power of their lost gods. Because he assumes an absence of historically conditioned skepticism, Campbell barely considers the possibility that our narrator's readers could have interpreted the loss of the

63. Ibid., 160.

64. *Ladeerzählungen*, 149, 181–86.

65. *VT* 14 (1964): 138.

66. *Ark Narrative*, 179–91.

ark differently from the way the narrator does—as a defeat of Yahweh.[67] He buys the narrator's interpretation so cheaply that he does not see that this interpretation is precisely the question at issue. Was Yahweh defeated? The narrator obviously says "No!", but could he have convinced his earliest readers—for whom the humiliation of defeat was still a recent memory—as easily as he has convinced Campbell?

To place this question in a context where it may be answered as objectively as possible, it is necessary to turn again to the comparative material dealing with the capture and return of divine images.[68] There is an abundance of primary source material on the subject, but in view of the discussions in Schicklberger,[69] Campbell,[70] Preuss,[71] and especially in the excellent new study of Morton Cogan,[72] we can keep our treatment relatively brief and concentrated on the underlying theology. Even so, some overlap will be unavoidable.

The practice of carrying off divine images is attested in cuneiform sources at least as early as the Old Babylonian period,[73] and it continued down to the end of the Neo-Babylonian state[74] and beyond. Part of the motivation behind such action was clearly economic—the images were often overlaid with gold or silver, decorated with precious or semiprecious

67. Ibid., 185–86.

68. The comparative mythological material having to do with the divine battle will be treated in the context of the discussion of 1 Sam 5:1–5.

69. *Ladeerzählungen*, 181–86.

70. *Ark Narrative*, 179–91.

71. H. D. Preuss, *Verspottung fremder Religionen im Alten Testament* (BWANT 12; Stuttgart: Kohlhammer, 1971), 43–49.

72. M. Cogan, *Imperialism and Religion: Assyria, Judah and Israel in the Eighth and Seventh Centuries B.C.E.* (SBLMS 19; Missoula, Mont.: SBL and Scholars Press, 1974), 9–41.

73. The question of the existence and use of divine statues in early Mesopotamia has been dealt with at length by Agnès Spycket, *Les statues dans les textes mesopotamiens des origines à la Ire dynastie de Babylone* (Cahiers de la Revue Biblique; Paris: Gabalda, 1968). Despite uncertainty for the earlier period, it is clear that Shu-ilishu of Isin (ca. 1984–1975 B.C., middle chronology) returned the statue of Nanna from Elam, where it had been carried earlier, after the fall of Ur, when the Ur III empire collapsed (Spycket, *Les statues*, 76).

74. See the so-called "Verse Account of Nabonidus," which praises Cyrus for returning the gods of Babylon to their own chapels, col. vi, 12–13 (Sidney Smith, *Babylonian Historical Texts Relating to the Capture and Downfall of Babylon* [London: Methuen, 1924], pl. X; translated in *ANET* [1955²], 315). In this case Nabonidus had apparently removed them to keep them out of the Persian's hands.

stones, and decked out in expensive finery—but one need not look far to find another, more theological motivation. The capture of the enemy's gods was seen, by the conquering power, as clear evidence for the superiority of the victor's gods. This is suggested by the common practice of dedicating the captured gods as booty to one's own gods,[75] a custom whose theological implications Esarhaddon makes quite explicit when he says, "The gods in whom they trusted I counted as booty."[76] Such a statement makes an interesting variant to the more normal characterization of the enemy as an impious man who trusted in himself,[77] and it raises the issue to the level

75. Note the repeated references to the practice in the bilingual of Hattusilis I from the Hittite Old Kingdom (*KBo* 10, 1:4–6, 18–20, *passim*). Assyrian references are numerous, but three examples should suffice. After conquering the land of Kutmuhi, Tiglath-pileser I boasted, "… sixty vessels of bronze, together with their gods, I dedicated unto Adad who loves me" (D. D. Luckenbill, *Ancient Records of Assyria and Babylonia* [Chicago: University of Chicago Press, 1926], 1:76). The same king treated the gods of Sugi in similar fashion: "I conquered the land of Sugi in its length and breadth and brought out twenty-five of their gods, their spoil, their goods, and their possessions.… At that time I presented the twenty-five gods of those lands, which I had captured with my hand and had taken away as gifts to the temple of Belit … and (to the temples) of Anu and Adad, and the Assyrian Ishtar.…" (Luckenbill, *ARAB*, 1:80). Adad-Nirari II followed the same pattern after his conquest of Kumane: "Their gods I placed before Assur, my lord, as gifts" (Luckenbill, *ARAB*, 1:117).

76. *ilâni*$^{\textit{meš}}$ *ti-ik-li-šú-nu šal-la-tiš am-nu*, Rykle Borger, *Die Inschriften Asarhaddons, Königs von Assyrien* (AfO Beiheft 9; Graz: Weidner, 1956), 58, episode 18:A, V 8. The same point was sometimes made by installing one's own deities in the captured territories. Shalmaneser III had his gods brought into the palaces of Giammu, a ruler in the Balih region who was murdered by his own subjects when the Assyrian army drew near (Luckenbill, *ARAB*, 1:222). Sargon II installed his gods in the city of Kisesim, which he renamed Kar-Nergal (A. G. Lie, *The Inscriptions of Sargon II, King of Assyria* [2 vols.; Paris: Geuthner, 1929], 1:16:93–95), and he set up the symbol of Ashur as the god of the captured Median districts that he renamed Kar-Sarruken (Lie, *Inscriptions*, 1:16:99).

77. Esarhaddon provides a good example of this motif as well: "And Sanduarri, the king of Kundu and Sissu, a dangerous enemy who did not respect my rule, whom the gods had deserted (*ša ilāni*$^{\textit{meš}}$ *ú-maš-šir-u-ma*), trusted in his steep mountains. He and Abdi-Milkutti, the king of Sidon, agreed to come to one another's aid and swore an oath to one another by their gods. They trusted in their own strength, but I trusted in Aššur, Sin, Šamaš, Bel, and Nabu, the great gods, my lords" (*ana emūqi rumānīšunu ittaklū anāku ana Aššur … attakilma*, Borger, *Asarhaddons*, 49–50, episode 6:A, III 20–29). It is found elsewhere in Esarhaddon (ibid., 41, episode 2:A, I 23–25); in Ashurbanipal (M. Streck, *Assurbanipal* [VAB 7/2; Leipzig: Hinrichs, 1916], 6, lines 55–56: … *ittakil ana emūq ramānīšu*, "Tarqu forgot the power of Assur, Istar, and the great gods my lords, and trusted in his own strength"; *passim*); in Sargon II, where Marduk-apaliddina is characterized as a wicked enemy who, trusting in the saltwater lagoon and the mass of the flood water (*eli ÍD marrati u gupuš edē ittakilma*), rebelled and ruled Babylon for twelve years against the will

of a confrontation between the gods. Unlike the more common motif that has the enemy's gods change sides of their own volition because of their former ward's sin,[78] this variant stresses the weakness of the enemy's gods over against one's own.[79] Occasionally the disparagement of the enemy's gods may even reach the point of effectively denying their divinity,[80] which may be expressed by smashing their images.[81] Such treatment is normally reserved for genuinely foreign deities,[82] but Sennacherib treated even the

---

of the gods (Lie, *Inscriptions* 1:42:263–73); in Tiglath-pileser III (Paul Rost, *Die Keilschrifttexte Tiglat-Pilesers III* [Leipzig: Pfeiffer, 1893], vol. 2, pl. 19:62); in the bilingual prayer of Tukulti-Ninurta I (*KAR* 128, rev. 3; translated in H. Gressmann, *Altorientalische Texte zum Alten Testament* [Berlin: de Gruyter, 1926²], 263–65); and elsewhere.

78. Note the Esarhaddon texts cited above (n. 77) and especially the following passage from the Tukulti-Ninurta Epic:

Against the oath-breaker Kaštiliaš the gods of heaven [and earth…
They showed […] against the king of the land and the peop[les…
They were angry with the *overseer*, their shepherd, and .[…
The Enlilship of the Lord of the Lands was distressed and […] Nippur.
So that he did not approach the dwelling of Dar-Kurigalzu ..[…
Marduk abandoned his lofty shrine, the city of .[…
He [cu]rsed his beloved city Kâr-.[…
Sin left Ur, [his…] town […
With Sippar and Larsa Ša[maš …
Ea […] Eridu, the House of Wisdom […
Ištaran was angry […
Anunitu does not approach Akkad […
The mistress of Uruk forsook […
The gods were wrath (*sic*) .[…

(W. G. Lambert, "Three Unpublished Fragments of the Tukulti Ninurta Epic," *AfO* 18 [1957]: 43–45:33–46).

Cogan regards this use of the divine abandonment motif by the victorious side a Neo-Assyrian development (*Imperialism and Religion*, 21), but its presence in the Tukulti-Ninurta Epic raises serious doubts about Cogan's late dating of the motif.

79. See 2 Kgs 18:30–35.

80. Ashurbanipal makes this quite explicit when he says of the captured Elamite gods, *ilānīšu ištarātīšu amnâ ana zaqiqī*, "I counted their gods and goddesses as powerless ghosts" (Streck, VAB 7/2], 54:64; see *CAD* z, 59).

81. Ashurbanipal did this to some of the Elamite gods: "I smashed their gods (*ušabbir ilānīšun*) and thereby soothed the heart of the lord of lords" (Streck, VAB 7/2], 50:119–20).

82. Since most such foreign gods had never been worked into the conqueror's theological system, they would normally lack the protective nimbus of awe with which traditional piety had clothed the native deities, and thus they were more exposed to harsh treatment.

Babylonian gods in a similar fashion.[83] Moreover, the act of returning the captured gods could also be used to underline the superiority of their captors, as Esarhaddon demonstrated when he inscribed the power of Ashur and his own name on the Arab gods before he returned them.[84]

The conquerors' theological interpretation of history was not always or necessarily self-evident to the vanquished, however. They normally attributed their defeat to the anger of their own gods, not to the power of the enemy's gods.[85] Sometimes the victor uses this theology of the defeated, in a slightly variant form, to claim divine approval for his actions,[86] particularly when the two sides share many of the same gods,[87] but it finds its purest form in the defeated's own accounts of the capture and return of their gods.

The oldest such account (assuming it is genuine)[88] is contained in a late copy of an inscription of the Kassite king Agum-kakrima.[89] The intent of this text, however, does not lie in the "explanation" it gives for Marduk's absence. Though this absence is probably linked to the earlier Hittite sacking of Babylon,[90] Agum-kakrima's inscription does not recount the "capture" of the divine image. In fact, it gives no explanation of why Marduk is away; the relevant portion of the text simply begins with the commandment of the great gods for Marduk to return to his city Babylon.[91] Marduk agrees, and Agum-kakrima is obedient to the

---

83. D. D. Luckenbill, *The Annals of Sennacherib* (Chicago: University of Chicago Press, 1925), 83:48.

84. Borger, *Asarhaddon,* 53, episode 14:A, IV 6–14.

85. This is how Israel usually explained her defeats, it is the explanation Mesha of Moab gave for Moab's losses to Israel ("Omri … oppressed Moab many days because Kemosh was angry against his land" [*ky y'np kmš b'rṣh*], *KAI* 1:181:5–6), and the same theology is reflected in the Mesopotamian texts to be discussed below.

86. See the Rabshakeh's clever use of this theology in his attempt to secure the surrender of Jerusalem. He suggests Hezekiah had angered Yahweh by his cultic innovations and that Yahweh (as a result?) had commanded the Assyrian to destroy Jerusalem (1 Kgs 8:22, 25).

87. See the passage from the Tukulti-Ninurta Epic cited above, in n. 78.

88. Landsberger considered it apocryphal (*MAOG* 4, 312; *JCS* 8, 68), but Weidner insisted that it was genuine (*AfO* 19, 138).

89. V *R* 33. For a partial translation of this text, see appendix A, text 1.

90. "Proclamation of Telepinus," col. i 29; text and translation in E. H. Sturtevant and G. Bechtel, *A Hittite Chrestomathy* (Philadelphia: Linguistic Society of America, 1935), 175–200; L. W. King, *Chronicles Concerning Early Babylonian Kings* (London: Luzac, 1907), 2:22:10.

91. Col. I, 44ff.

divine purpose.[92] After making the appropriate divinatory inquiries from Shamash, the Kassite king sends to the distant land of Hani, takes Marduk and Sarpanitum by the hand, and returns them to Babylon.[93] The remainder of the long text—by far the major portion—describes the refurbishing and decoration of the restored images and the redecoration and beautification of their sanctuaries, before ending with a typical curse and blessing formula.

A far greater concern for the theological interpretation of history is found in a group of texts dating from the period of Nebuchadnezzar I's Elamite war. Perhaps the most interesting of these is the "Prophecy of Marduk," recently reedited by Rykle Borger.[94] This text has Marduk narrate past history in autobiographical form down to the time of Nebuchadnezzar's Elamite campaign. Then, either as genuine prophecy or, as *vaticinia ex eventu,* he predicts Nebuchadnezzar's victory over Elam and the good days to come. The emphasis in the recitation of the past, as far as the often fragmentary text allows one to judge, is on the earlier "trips" of Marduk's statue. Mursilis's capture and removal of Marduk's statue becomes a self-motivated business trip utilized by Marduk to establish trade connections between Babylon and Hatti.

> *aqbi ana māt Ḫatti allik Ḫatti aš'al kussi Anūtīya ina libbīša addi 24 šanāti ina libbīša ašbākūma ḫarrānāt mārī. Bābili ina libbīša ukīn.*
>
> I gave the command. I went to the land of Hatti. I questioned Hatti. The throne of my Anu-ship I set up within it. I dwelt within it for 24 years, and I established within it the caravan trade of the Babylonians.[95]

A sojourn in Assyria, no doubt reflecting Tuklulti-Ninurta's removal of the Marduk statue following his victory over Kashtiliash, is also mentioned, but the reason for this trip is obscured by a break.[96] Marduk's favorable treatment of Assyria, however, suggests it was presented as a peaceful visit.[97]

---

92. Col. I, 51–II 7.

93. Col. II 8–17.

94. Rykle Borger, "Gott Marduk und Gott-König Sulgi als Propheten, Zwei prophetische Texte," *Bibliotheca Orientalis* 28 (1971): 3–24.

95. Ibid., 5:13–19.

96. Ibid., 6, the beginning lines of K 7065.

97. Ibid., 7:12'.

Nevertheless, Marduk makes it clear that he was in charge of the situation; he may have gone away on trips, but he always returned.

> *anāku Marduk bēlu rabû bēl u purussê anākuma mannu isbat ḫarrāna annīta* ^{KI} *(ki? ašar?) alliku aḫḫisa.*
>
> I am Marduk the great lord. I alone am lord of destinies and decisions. Who has taken this road? Wherever I went, from there I returned.[98]

This strong affirmation of Marduk's control of history, following the recitation of past events involving the removal of Marduk's statue from Babylon, prepares the stage for the god's interpretation of a more recent disaster, one still too productive of existential angst to be easily dismissed as a business trip—the Elamite conquest of Babylon and plunder of Marduk's statue. Marduk does not refer to the event as a defeat. Indeed, Marduk asserts that he himself gave the command for his departure from Babylon as well as for Babylon's subsequent misfortunes, but he "doth protest too much."

> *[anā]ku aqbi ana māt Elamti allikma illikū ilū kalâma anākuma aqbi nindabê bīltāti anākuma aprus.*
>
> I myself gave the command. I went to the land of Elam, and all the gods went with me—I alone gave the command. The food offerings of the temples I alone cut off.[99]

Why is Marduk so insistent, unless there were those who questioned this interpretation of history? Like Yahweh in Second Isaiah,[100] Marduk in this text cites earlier historical events to lend credence to his interpretation of this more recent event and to his promise for the future. But just as the Israelite prophet's interpretation of history did not always go unchallenged,[101] so, reading between the lines, did Marduk's version of the past have its detractors. Interestingly enough, the other texts dealing with

---

98. Ibid., 7:18'–21'.

99. Ibid., 7:21'–24'.

100. Isa 41:21–29; 44:6–8; 45:20–21; 48:3–8.

101. There are indications that Second Isaiah's message was received with skepticism—note his constant references to Israel's deafness, blindness, and obstinacy—and even persecution (51:5–7), but the classic example is the rival interpretation of history the Judean women threw into the teeth of Jeremiah (Jer 44:15–19).

Nebuchadnezzar I's Elamite war and Marduk's return from Elam all date from the period after Nebuchadnezzar's victory, and while they are still concerned to interpret the events, they seem less troubled by doubt. In one of these,[102] a fragmentary historical epic, Nebuchadnezzar prays to Marduk,[103] calls his attention to the lamentations of his people,[104] asks him, "How long will you, the lord of Babylon, live in an enemy country?" and implores him, "Turn your face to Esangil which you love."[105] Whereupon Marduk hears Nebuchadnezzar's prayer,[106] commands the king to take him back to Babylon,[107] and promises to give Elam to Nebuchadnezzar.[108] Unfortunately, the text breaks off at this point.

We also possess two large fragments of one or two closely related bilingual compositions dealing with the same historical event. The first, which has been edited and discussed by Lambert,[109] begins with the praise of a god, probably Marduk.[110] Then the earthly king, his appointee, continues with a first-person narration.[111] At the time of a former king, there was disorder in the land, good departed, evil became regular, and, as a result, Marduk grew angry and commanded the gods to desert Babylon.[112] The wicked Elamites took advantage of the ensuing helplessness of the country to carry off the divine images and ruin the shrines,[113] but Marduk observed everything and was displeased.[114] At this point the first fragment ends. The second,[115] which may be a later continuation of the same text, begins with what appears to be the end of an account of Marduk's devastation of Elam.[116] Then, in response to the king's constant

102. *CT* 13, 48. See appendix, text 2.
103. Line 4.
104. Lines 6–7.
105. Lines 8, 10.
106. Line 11.
107. Line 17.
108. Line 18.
109. Wilfred G. Lambert, "Enmeduranki and Related Matters," *JCS* 21 (1967): 126–38; text (i).
110. Lines 1–6.
111. Lines 7ff.
112. Lines 15–18.
113. Lines 23–24.
114. Lines 25ff.
115. IV *R* 20, No. *1; BA* V, 339ff. See appendix, text 3.
116. Lines 1–5.

prayer, Marduk became merciful, left the wickedness of Elam, and took a joyous road back to Babylon.[117] The people of the land stared in joyous admiration of his lofty stature as the jubilant procession led to Marduk's lordly cella, where sacrifices were then offered in great abundance.[118]

Apparently the same event is also reflected in a fragmentary hymn,[119] presumably to Marduk.[120] After an initial break of at least five lines, the text has a hymnic introduction referring to the god in the third person.[121] It describes how the god, in accordance with his merciful character, heard the narrator's prayer and grew calm.[122] Then, switching to direct address of the deity, the writer praises Marduk by recounting how the god destroyed the Elamite who did not reverence his divinity.[123] Unfortunately, the end of the tablet is also badly damaged, so it is impossible to tell if it related Marduk's return to Babylon.

Moving to the later period, it is hard to find any event of the first millennium more pregnant with theological implications than Sennacherib's total devastation of Babylon. His almost unparalleled desecration of native Mesopotamian gods—some of which he carried away,[124] but others of

117. Lines 6–12.

118. Lines 16ff.

119. DT 71; copy in *BA* V, 386ff. It is possible that the text is later and should be connected to Ashurbanipal's defeat of the Elamites. See the discussion and references in Manfred Weippert, "'Heiliger Krieg' in Israel und Assyrien," *ZAW* 84 (1972): 482 n. 108. See appendix, text 4.

120. The name of the deity does not occur on the preserved part of the text, so as Weippert points out (*ZAW* 84, 482 n. 109), it is not certain that the hymn was addressed to Marduk. Nevertheless, if one adopts the Nebuchadnezzar I date, which is supported by the hymn's resemblance to the other texts celebrating the success of Nebuchadnezzar I, that same similarity would argue for Marduk.

121. Lines 5–9.

122. Lines 9–13.

123. Lines 14ff.

124. Sennacherib himself does not mention this, but it seems to be presupposed by the later inscriptions of Esarhaddon, Ashurbanipal, and Nabonidus. It is possible, however, that the divine images returned to Babylon were actually brand new ones made in Assyrian workshops. See Benno Landsberger, *Brief des Bischofs von Esagila an König Asarhaddon* (Medelingen der Koninklijke Nederlandse Akademie van Wetenschappen, AFD. Letterkunde, Nieuwe Reeks, 28/6; Amsterdam, 1965), 20–27; and A. K. Grayson, "Chronicles and the Akitu Festival," *Actes de la XVIIe Rencontre Assyriologique Internationale* (Brussels, 1970), 160–70.

which he simply smashed or threw into the canal[125]—produced a spate of theological explanations. According to his own inscriptions, Sennacherib attempted to blot out all memory of Babylon and its temples.[126] Such an action could hardly be justified without divine sanction. Sennacherib's inscriptions make it clear that the move was undertaken in response to Ashur's command, to soothe the imperial god's anger,[127] and not simply out of human spite. Another text that was previously (erroneously) thought to contain an account of Marduk's resurrection also attempts to give a theological justification for Sennacherib's actions.[128] This remarkable piece of religio-political propaganda, no doubt commissioned by the Assyrian king, reinterprets ritual events during the Akitu festival to represent a trial of Marduk for rebelling against Ashur.[129]

Royal support or not, Sennacherib's official interpretation could not win universal acceptance even in Assyria, where Marduk had long been worshiped alongside Ashur.[130] With the rise of the pro-Babylonian party under Esarhaddon, a new theological explanation had to be offered. It seems to have been derived from the Babylonians themselves, though adapted for the use of the Assyrian crown.[131] Under the rule of a former king, so the new explanation stated, the Babylonians became wicked and provoked Marduk to punish them.[132] Without mentioning Sennacherib, his devastation of Babylon was attributed directly to Marduk, who none-

---

125. Luckenbill, *Sennacherib*, 83–84:48–52.

126. Ibid., 84:53–54.

127. Ibid., 137:37; 138:44ff.

128. *KAR* 143 and 219; W. von Soden, "Gibt es ein Zeugnis dass die Babylonier an Marduks Wiederauferstehung glaubten?" *ZA* NF *17* (1955): 130–66; idem, "Ein neues Bruchstück des assyrischen Kommentars zum Marduk-Ordal," *ZA* NF 18 (1957): 224–34; J. N. Postgate, "Two Marduk Ordeal Fragments," *ZA* NF 60 (1970): 124–27; J. N. Postgate, *The Governor's Palace Archive* (Cuneiform Texts from Nimrud 2; British School of Archaeology in Iraq, 1973), no. 268.

129. See the most recent treatment by Thorkild Jacobsen *in Unity and Diversity: Essays in the History, Literature, and Religion of the Ancient Near East* (ed. H. Goedicke and J. J. M. Roberts; Baltimore: Johns Hopkins University Press, 1975), 73–74.

130. His cult is attested to in Ashur from at least the ninth century (A. Schott, "Die Anfänge Marduks als eines assyrischen Gottes," *ZA* NF 9 [1936]: 318–21) and perhaps as early as the fourteenth century B.C. (O. Edzard, "Mesopotamien," *Wörterbuch der Mythologie* (ed. H. W. Haussig; Stuttgart: Klett, 1965], 1:96; E. Weidner, "Studien zur Zeitgeschichte Tukulti-Ninurtas I.," *AfO* 13 [1939/40]: 119–21).

131. Cogan, *Imperialism and Religion*, 21.

132. Borger, *Asarhaddon*, 12–14, episodes 2–5.

theless relented after only eleven years of the threatened seventy-year punishment had passed.[133] Marduk simply altered the order of the wedges on the tablet, turning seventy into eleven, and then issued a command to the new Assyrian king to rebuild Babylon.[134] Esarhaddon claims to have accomplished the task, and inscriptions commissioned by him tell of the refurbishing of the divine images and the return of the divine statues to their newly restored shrines.[135] The ritual procession that supposedly marked the return of some of these images from the workshops in Assyria to their sanctuaries in Babylon is worth noting. From Ashur to the quay of Babylon, brushwood piles were lit every third of a mile, and every double mile they slaughtered fat bulls.[136]

In actual fact, however, Esarhaddon died before he could carry out the festive procession described in his inscriptions. It was left to his son, Ashurbanipal, to fulfill the somewhat premature press releases. After his brother Šamaš-šum-ukīn, his co-ruler in Babylon, had carefully consulted the Babylonian gods,[137] Ashurbanipal returned Marduk to Babylon in his first full regnal year.[138] Faithful to his father's plans, Ashurbanipal describes the procession in language very similar to that used by his father's overzealous scribes.[139] From the quay of Ashur to the quay of Babylon, sacrifices were offered, brush piles and torches were lit to give light for every double mile, and Ashurbanipal's whole army surrounded Marduk making music day and night.[140] One can hardly make this procession into a regular ritual, since Ashurbanipal states that Marduk had settled in Ashur during the reign of a previous king but had returned to Babylon during his own reign[141]—a statement that points toward a historically unique event.

---

133. Ibid., 14–15, episodes 6–10.

134. Ibid., 15–18, episodes 10–15.

135. Ibid., 19–25, episodes 16–36.

136. Ibid., 88–89, especially lines 18–20.

137. We have two relatively complete reports of such inquiries preserved in J. A. Knudtzon's *Assyrische Gebete an den Sonnengott für Staat und königliches Haus aus der Zeit Asarhaddons und Asurbanipals* (Leipzig: Pfeiffer, 1893), nos. 104 + 105 and 149. Both were apparently taken on the 23rd of Nisan, 668 B.C., i.e., shortly after the beginning of Ashurbanipal's first full year of reign. See appendix, texts 5 and 6.

138. Streck, VAB 7/2, 263:26.

139. Ibid., 265–69.

140. Ibid., 265–67.

141. Ibid., 245:36–44.

One should note in passing that, while Ashurbanipal attributed the destruction of Babylon to Marduk's anger,[142] alongside this view is a more ambiguous interpretation that says that Marduk, during the reign of a former king, went to live with his father in Ashur.[143] Though compatible with Marduk's voluntary destruction of his own city, this motif moves toward the earlier view of Sennacherib in underscoring Marduk's subordination to Ashur.

Much later—long after Assyria had passed from the scene—Nabonidus picked up the same Babylonian theological explanation of Babylon's fall adapted by the Assyrian court, but he carried it further than did his Assyrian predecessors.[144] Unlike Esarhaddon and Ashurbanipal, who refused to castigate Sennacherib explicitly, the Neo-Babylonian king makes it clear that the Assyrian was guilty of sacrilege. Marduk was angry with his people, and the Assyrian dealt with Babylon according to Marduk's anger.[145] He destroyed the sanctuaries, ruined the cult, and took Marduk to Ashur, where the god made his home until his anger had passed.[146] When Marduk's anger had passed, however, he remembered his lordly dwelling and began to take vengeance.[147] The guilty Assyrian king was murdered by his own son.[148] Following a short break in the tablet, Nabonidus goes on to tell how Marduk raised up the Ummanmanda to take revenge on Ashur and its gods.[149] Moreover, Nabonidus, who was just as devoted to many of the Assyrian gods as to Marduk, very interestingly disassociates himself from these actions of Marduk. They were the work of Marduk and the Ummanmanda, but the great gods should know that Nabonidus had no part in this sacrilege.[150] Nabonidus obviously sought to escape the avenging wrath of the wronged gods. He had learned the lesson which the late history of Assyria had taught. Although the punishment might be delayed, the sacrilege of a Sennacherib—what-

142. Ibid., 263:29.

143. Ibid., 244:37–41.

144. Stephen Langdon, *Die neubabylonischen Königsinschriften* (VAB 4; Leipzig: Hinrichs, 1912), 270ff., Nabonid no. 8; translated in *ANET* (1955^2), 308–11.

145. Ibid., i 18–19.

146. Ibid., i 1–25.

147. Ibid., i 26–41.

148. Ibid., i 39–41.

149. Ibid., ii 1–31.

150. Ibid., ii 33–41.

ever his nationality and whatever his religious motivation—would not go unpunished.

Conclusion

This sketch of the theology of the divine image has been kept to a minimum. We have discussed only selected material that directly relates to the capture and/or return of the divine images. Nevertheless, this sketch should prove helpful in the exegetical discussion of the following chapters. In the first place, it should forever squelch the oft-repeated assertion that the Philistines would not have returned the ark,[151] that such an action is "unglaubwürdig,"[152] that it "widerspricht allen Erfahrungen der Vergangenheit und Gegenwart."[153] The Assyrians, and presumably the Hittites, did return captured deities, even without the pressure of a plague. Moreover, such transfers of the divine symbol were preceded, just as in the ark narrative, by a careful consultation of the omens.

In the second place, one must now question the widespread tendency to regard 2 Sam 6 as the reflex of a regular temple liturgy.[154] Such an interpretation runs counter to the parallels where the similar, historical return of an image to its sanctuary is accompanied by ritual practices analogous to those mentioned in the ark narrative. Just as Ashurbanipal's army participated in the return of Marduk to his new sanctuary, so David's army participated in the return of the ark of Yahweh.[155] Just as Marduk's journey was accompanied by music and rejoicing, so was the ark's.[156] Moreover, just as the Assyrians offered sacrifices every double mile from the quay of Ashur to the quay of Babylon, so David offered an ox and a fatling after

151. W. H. Kosters, "De verhalen over de ark in Samuel," *Theologische Tijdschrift* (1893): 361–78; S. Mowinckel, *Psalmenstudien II* (Videnskapsselskapets Skrifter, 2. Hist.-Filos. Klasse 1921/6; Kristiania: Dybwad, 1922), 113 n. 1; Gustav Hölscher, *Die Anfänge der hebraischen Geschichtsschreibung* (Sitzungsberichte der Heidelberger Akademie der Wissenschaften, Philosophisch-historische Klasse 1941/43, 3; Heidelberg: Winter, 1942), 75 n.1; H. Gressmann, SAT 2/1, 15.

152. Hölscher, *Die Anfänge*, 75 n. 1.

153. Gressmann, SAT 2/1, 15.

154. Mowinckel, *The Psalms in Israel's Worship*, 1:175–76.

155. 2 Sam 6:1.

156. 2 Sam 6:5, 14–15.

every six steps.[157] In view of these parallels, de Vaux's explanation for the cultic character of 2 Sam 6 is more to the point than perhaps even he realized: "Le caractere du recit s'explique suffisamment si l'on considere que le transfert de l'arche par David est lui-meme un acte cultuel....[158]

Finally, and perhaps most important of all, the treatment accorded plundered images raised serious questions about the captured gods' control of history.[159] The conqueror answered these questions one way, while the defeated, when the bitterness of defeat had passed, saw the answer differently. Once the god had been recaptured or returned, it was not too difficult to look at the disaster in the receding past as imposed by the anger of the now favorably disposed god himself. Such theological certainty was far less assured in the immediate aftermath of defeat, or when the recent return of the image had been anything but glorious. The self-assurance of the conqueror and the apparent historical verification of his gods' authority sometimes made the official theology of the defeated problematic. The very few theological treatments of the past originating in such periods of

157. 2 Sam 6:13. This verse is usually interpreted to mean that after the first six steps, when nothing bad happened, David offered a sacrifice, and the procession proceeded on without more to do, but W. R. Arnold had already pointed to the correct interpretation in 1917: "The editor's meaning is that an ox and a fatling were sacrificed at every six paces of the march" *(Ephod and Ark: A Study in the Records and Religion of the Ancient Hebrews* [Harvard Theological Studies 3; Cambridge: Harvard University Press, 1917], 41). Hertzberg saw the possibility of this interpretation, but he dismissed it without a second thought, "natürlich ist die Meinung nicht: alle sechs Schritte!" (*Die Samuelbücher* [ATD 10; Göttingen: Vandenhoeck & Ruprecht, 1968^4], 229). Why is that so obvious? If the Assyrians could offer sacrifices all the way from Ashur to Babylon—a quite considerable distance—why could David not offer sacrifices every six steps from the house of Obed-edom to Jerusalem? The location of Obed-edom's house is unknown, but it could not have been far from Jerusalem and may have been in its immediate vicinity. Even so, such a procedure would certainly have required a large number of sacrificial animals, but that is presupposed by verse 19, and such largess corresponds with Solomon's later practice on a similar occasion (1 Kgs 8:5, 62–64).

158. R. de Vaux, *Les livres de Samuel* (La Sainte Bible; Paris: Cerf, 1961), 167b.

159. The author of the Epistle of Jeremiah was merely exploiting a long latent problem when he cited the treatment of divine images as an argument against idolatry (1:15, 48–49, 56–58 [Baruch 6:15, 48–49, 56–58]), but his argument had a double edge that he failed to grasp. Essentially the same problem confronted Israel in an only slightly more attenuated form. Note, for example, how the author of the Syriac Apocalypse of Baruch goes to great pains to preserve the sacred objects from the enemy (6:1–10) and to insist that it was God, not the enemy, who destroyed Jerusalem (5:3; 7:1–8:2), while even that is softened by the assertion that the Jerusalem destroyed was not the real Jerusalem (4:2–7).

uncertainty reflect, by their very insistence on the native god's absolute control of events, the underlying doubt against which such accounts are written.

2
THE EXTENT OF THE NARRATIVE

One of the major problems in analyzing the ark narrative is determining its scope. Where does it begin, where does it end, and what secondary accretions must be removed from the narrative? The last of these questions we will treat in the following exegetical sections, but the questions concerning the beginning and the end of the narrative cannot wait.

The Beginning

Since Rost's fundamental study, most scholars have pointed to 1 Sam 4:1b as the beginning of the narrative.[1] Recently, however, this view has been challenged by John Willis, who argues strongly for the unity and homogeneity of 1 Sam 1–7.[2] While we are not convinced by Willis's analysis, it is one that must be given careful consideration. It is at least clear, as he has pointed out,[3] that 1 Sam 4:1b–7:1 is an incomplete narrative, apart from some relationship to some of the material contained in the preceding chapters. A number of Willis's arguments parallel our own, and the reader is also referred to his discussion.

To begin with, it is difficult to regard 1 Sam 4:1b as a natural beginning for the following, supposedly independent, complete, and self-contained narrative. Too many questions are left unanswered. Why, for instance, are the Israelites defeated? That the Israelites do not know the reason creates no difficulty—a similar motif occurs elsewhere (in the story of the defeat at Ai, for example)[4]—but that the reader—or hearer, as the case may be—is

1. See the summary of later views in Campbell, *Ark Narrative*, 28–54.

2. "An Anti-Elide Narrative Tradition from a Prophetic Circle at the Ramah Sanctuary," *JBL* 90 (1971): 288–308.

3. Ibid., 300.

4. Josh 7:1–9.

given no explanation for this unexpected course of events is quite strange. There are few, if any, analogies for such a narrative technique in the Old Testament, and whatever analogies might be cited seem to be cancelled out when the writer adds a second defeat involving the loss of the ark and the death of the priests of Yahweh. Where else in Old Testament literature does one simply narrate such a devastating blow to Israelite piety without any attempt at theological explanation? Moreover, who are Eli, Hophni, and Phinehas? The narrator introduces them in 4:4 as though they were already well-known by the reader. This would seem to imply the existence of a preceding narrative about them.[5] It has also been suggested, though this is not absolutely necessary, that Eli's anxiety over the ark in 4:13 presupposes a similarly missing background.[6]

In other words, to make the ark narrative a complete, self-contained unit, one must supplement Rost's text with a tradition introducing the main characters and alerting the reader to Yahweh's displeasure toward Israel. The tradition of the wickedness of Eli's sons (1 Sam 2:12–17, 22–25) would fill part of that need. It would explain the reason for Yahweh's anger and, in particular, why his anger reached even the priests and led to the loss of Israel's most sacred cult object. It would also be an adequate introduction to the sons of Eli, though one would still lack an introduction to Eli himself. One must question whether that part of the original ark narrative may be reconstructed from the present text of Samuel. It would appear that the original beginning of the ark narrative has been fragmented and partly lost by the secondary insertion of the traditions about Samuel's childhood.

This is where we differ from Willis. He regards the present form of 1 Sam 1–7, including the Samuel traditions, as an original, integral unity.[7] Though his analysis is suggestive for interpreting the present form of the text, such unity it now possesses is clearly redactional, not original. Considering the major role Samuel plays in the present form of 1 Sam 1–3, the total omission of any mention of him in 4:1b–7:1 is certainly striking—particularly since 3:21 states that Yahweh continued to reveal himself to

5. As noted already by H. P. Smith, *The Books of Samuel* (ICC: Edinburgh: T&T Clark, 1899), xx.

6. R. Press, "Der Prophet Samuel: Eine traditions-geschichtliche Untersuchung," *ZAW* 56 (1938): 181.

7. *JBL* 90 (1971): 289.

the now famous Samuel in Shilo—and suggests that these two sections in their present form could not be an original unity. Willis attempts to overcome this argument by pointing to a literary analogy between 1 Sam 1–7 and several other texts.[8] According to Willis, each of these texts reflects the same literary pattern: (1) "the writer tells how Yahweh prepares a man to lead Israel through some crisis" (Samuel, 1 Sam 1:1–4:1a; Jephthah, Judg 11:1–3; Samson, Judg 13:2–25; Saul, 1 Sam 9–10; David, 1 Sam 16); (2) "he describes this crisis" (Samuel, 1 Sam 4:1b–7:1; Jephthah, Judg 11:4–28; Samson, Judg 14:1–18; 15:1–6, 9–13; 16:1–27; Saul, 1 Sam 11:1–4; David, 1 Sam 17:1–30); (3) "and finally he relates the successful manner in which that man guides Israel through the crisis" (Samuel, 1 Sam 7:2–17; Jephthah, Judg 11:29–33; Samson, Judg 14:19–20; 15:7–18, 14–20; 16:28–31; Saul, 1 Sam 11:5–11; David, 1 Sam 17:31–54).[9] A close examination of these supposed analogies, however, merely strengthens the impression that Samuel's absence in 1 Sam 4:1b–7:1 is peculiar. Only in this one case is the hero missing from the "description of the crisis." Jephthah appears in the second and every succeeding verse of his corresponding section except verses 16–27, which contain a speech of Jephthah's. Samson occurs in either the first or second verse of his "description of the crisis" sections, and both Saul and David appear in their corresponding sections. In short, Willis has provided no analogy for the omission of Samuel's name in this section; his evidence suggests rather that 1 Sam 4:1b–7:1 was not originally part of any such literary pattern. Such a judgment is also strengthened by the observation that 1 Sam 5–7:1 has already resolved the crisis presented in 1 Sam 4. Yahweh has already defeated the Philistines without Samuel's help, and to introduce it at this point actually works as an anticlimax. It is possibly this reason as much as historical consideration that moved the redactor to insert 7:2, thus providing a temporal and literary separation between 4:1b–7:1 and the following Samuel story.

One other point should be made against Willis's analysis. He argues that the narrative in 1 Sam 1–4 contrasts Samuel and Eli (much as the later material in Samuel contrasts Saul and David) and thus prepares the way for Samuel to assume the leadership that Eli relinquished.[10] It is not at all clear from the narrative, however, that Samuel replaced Eli. The role

8. Ibid., 298.
9. Ibid., 298–99.
10. Ibid., 290–92.

of Eli is constantly given as *kwhn*, "priest," not *šwpṭ*, "judge,"[11] and according to 1 Sam 7:1 it was not Samuel, but Eleazar, the son of Abinadab, who replaced Eli as priest of the ark.[12]

Our analysis, in contrast to Willis's, is unaffected by the absence of Samuel from 4:1b–7:1, because we assume that the Samuel figure is also secondary to the earlier Eli material contained in 1 Sam 1–3. Though the Samuel material has been cleverly interwoven with this primary Eli narrative, the redactor has not succeeded in completely integrating the two corpora. Clear pointers to the secondary character of this interweaving remain. He has successfully related Samuel to Eli, but not to Eli's sons, where the relationship remains very superficial. The account of the wickedness of Eli's sons in 2:12–17, 22–25, though bracketed and separated by references to Samuel, stands apart from the Samuel material and would read quite smoothly if the intervening verses were simply deleted.

Even more instructive is a comparison of the anti-Elide prophecy of the unnamed man of God (2:27–36) with the subsequent prophecy of Samuel in chapter 3. The two prophecies are so similar that one is clearly redundant, dependent on the other. Willis correctly observed that "3:12 assumes the existence of, and explicitly refers to, 2:27–36,"[13] but he failed to draw the obvious conclusion from this fact. The oracle of the anonymous prophet existed prior to the insertion of the Samuel material and was adapted by the later redactor for the glorification of his boy hero. Thus 2:27–36 should probably be included with 2:12–17, 22–25 as part of the material presupposed by 1 Sam 4:1b–7:1. The connection with the fall of Abiathar (1 Kgs 2:27) is a secondary interpretation of this oracle, though it may have led to some retouching.[14]

To summarize, the redactor responsible for inserting the Samuel material had before him traditions concerning Eli and his wicked sons—traditions that knew nothing of Samuel but only of an unnamed man of God. Samuel was fitted into this preexisting material by working Eli into an originally independent birth story, which was then placed before the account of the wickedness of Eli's sons. This latter material was preserved

11. The sole exception in 1 Sam 4:18 is characterized by its schematic form as a Deuteronomistic addition.

12. See below.

13. *JBL* 90 (1971): 293.

14. See below.

largely as it stood; the redactor merely inserted references to Samuel at key points to highlight the contrast between the lad and the sons of Eli. Finally, to clinch the matter, the redactor rephrased the oracle of chapter 2, attributing its rewording to Samuel, to prepare the way for Samuel's rise to prominence as a prophet of God.

If the preceding case for the secondary character of the Samuel material is allowed, the other arguments for separating 4:1b–7:1 from 2:12–17, 22–25, 27–36 carry very little weight. Some have argued that 1 Sam 4:1b–22 paints a favorable portrait of the Elides in contrast to the unfavorable portrait in 1 Sam 2:12–17, 22–25, and 27–36.[15] It has even been suggested that Hophni and Phinehas are heroic figures who try to save Israel by carrying the ark into battle.[16] That is surely an exaggeration. Although 1 Sam 4 treats Eli sympathetically as a tragic figure, the treatment of Hophni and Phinehas is at best neutral. Such treatment does not constitute a contrast to 1 Sam 2:12–17, 22–25. Even in this earlier passage, Eli, the upright but overly permissive father, is a tragic but sympathetic figure.

Schicklberger maintains further that the death of the Elides in 1 Sam 4 is not meant to be understood as a punishment.[17] But this is to misunderstand the whole movement of the story. It is precisely because of the relation to 1 Sam 2 that their death does not have to be so characterized. The point of it is clear from the preceding chapter. Once the wickedness of Eli's sons has been established, there is no need for the account of their punishment to do more than coldly narrate the facts. The structurally significant role of Hophni and Phinehas[18] can only be explained in light of the judgment of doom against the house of Eli in 1 Sam 2. The intense interest in their death makes sense only in that context. The attention accorded Phinehas's wife is not motivated by sympathy toward her husband; it merely serves to highlight the fall of the Elides and the national tragedy involved in the loss of the ark.

Finally, we must refer to the most recent arguments of Campbell in behalf of the discontinuity of 1 Sam 1–3 and 4–6. He maintains that the catastrophe of 1 Sam 4 is of national dimension, whereas the threat against the Elides is personal and in no way commensurate with the defeat of the

15. Schicklberger, *Ladeerzählungen*, 62 and n. 135.

16. J. Dus, "Die Erzählung über den Verlust der Lade, 1 Sam. IV," *VT* (1963): 334.

17. *Ladeerzählungen*, 62.

18. See below.

nation as a whole.[19] But this is to ignore the central role of these priests in the life of the nation and in relation to the ark. It is not difficult to assume that their death would be meted out in the context of their duties and that Israel might endure tragedy as a consequence.

Further, Campbell argues from silence that mention should have been made in 1 Sam 4 of the fulfillment of the prophecies of judgment in 1 Sam 1–3.[20] But once again such an argument from silence can hardly be said to carry much weight, particularly in this case. The proximity of the presentation of the fulfillment to the prophecy itself requires no additional comment. Once again the strategically placed comments about Hophni and Phinehas in 1 Sam 4 make the point clearly. As an analogy, one may cite Samuel's prophecy to Saul in 1 Sam 28:16–19. When the narrator finally gets to the fulfillment of this prophecy three chapters later (in 1 Sam 31), he similarly fails to call his readers' attention to the fact that the prophecy has now been fulfilled, but no one doubts that these two passages are so related, Moreover, one must question whether the kind of "fulfillment notation" Campbell expects is at all common outside the editorial comments of the Deuteronomistic Historian.

The End

After the preceding discussion, one may quickly dismiss Willis's attempt to find the end of the narrative in 1 Sam 7.[21] The connections he notes between 4:1b–7:1 and 7:2–17 can be adequately explained by assuming that the redactor responsible for introducing this material had 2:12–17, 22–25, 27–36; 4:1b–7:1 before him and thus, as with the birth and childhood stories, could shape his material to create links.

Second Sam 6 must be taken more seriously as a candidate for the conclusion of the ark narrative. Though a number of scholars have disagreed with Rost, his proposal that 1 Sam 4–6 and 2 Sam 6 make up a single entity has been widely accepted. Most of the dissertations written on this material over the last two decades have agreed with Rost.[22] Schicklberger is a notable and important exception. Our study of the material has

19. Campbell, *Ark Narrative*, 175.

20. Ibid.

21. *JBL* 90 (1971): 302–5.

22. See Campbell, *Ark Narrative*, 28–54.

led us to agree with Schicklberger, who disagrees with Rost and those who maintain an original relationship between 1 Sam 4–6 and 2 Sam 6, including, most recently, Campbell.[23] Some of our arguments have to do with the historical setting and intention of the narrative in 1 Sam 4–6. Those will be mentioned in the context of our discussion of that matter later on. In this context we will simply rehearse very briefly the literary-critical reasons for viewing 1 Sam 4–6 and 2 Sam 6 separately.[24]

Rost has pointed to a similarity in vocabulary between 1 Sam 4–6 and 2 Sam 6.[25] But, like most of Rost's stylistic arguments, this one is quite weak. Of the more than fifty words that Rost lists in his vocabulary analysis, only four appear in both 1 Sam 4–6 and 2 Sam 6.[26] The shared vocabulary is not particularly distinctive, considering the general similarity of the events being narrated, and it could be explained just as easily by making 2 Sam 6 a later addition, dependent on the material in 1 Sam 4–6. The methodological fuzziness and uselessness of such a list as Rost's is pointed out clearly by Campbell.[27]

If one follows Rost in assuming that the narrative is completely preserved, there are serious problems in moving from 1 Sam 7:1 to 2 Sam 6:1. There is a definite break. Kiryath-yearim in the first passage is called Baalath-judah in the second. Even if these designate the same places (and this is questionable),[28] it is not likely that in the same narrative the name should suddenly shift after it has been clearly established.[29] Further, Eleazar of 1 Sam 4–6 is replaced without explanation by Uzzo and Ahyo. We note further, as have Schicklberger and others,[30] that the style and form of these two narratives is different. One may compare 2 Sam 6 to the his-

23. Ibid., 169–74.

24. Schicklberger gives a more extensive discussion (*Ladeerzählungen*, 129–49). For that reason we do not go into great detail here.

25. Leonhard Rost, *Die Überlieferung von der Thronnachfolge Davids* (BWANT 3/6; Stuttgart: Kohlhammer, 1926), 14–23 = *Das Kleine Credo und andere Studien zum Alten Testament* (Heidelberg: Quelle & Meyer,1965), 130–38.

26. Campbell, *Ark Narrative*, 43.

27. Ibid., 43–44. Though Campbell in this passage is really defending Rost against Schunck's criticism, he can do this only by dismissing the argument Rost made from vocabulary statistics.

28. See the long discussion in Schicklberger, *Ladeerzählungen*, 133–40.

29. 1 Chr 13:5 is a later narrative that cannot be used to account for the two names. See Schicklberger, *Ladeerzählungen*, 133–40.

30. Ibid., 144–49.

torical chronicles that record the return of despoiled images by victorious monarchs.[31] Yahweh and the ark are no longer the main actors; they must share the limelight with David, who takes the initiative for transferring the ark to Jerusalem.

There are, nonetheless, clear connections between 2 Sam 6 and 1 Sam 4–7:1. The conception of the ark's awesome power is described similarly in both, and it is found in the same household, that of Abinadab. Schicklberger,[32] following Vriezen and others,[33] explains these links between 1 Sam 4–7:1 and 2 Sam 6 by making 1 Sam 4–7:1 dependent on the older narrative in 2 Sam 6. We cannot follow him in this assumption. His arguments for this direction of dependency are unconvincing. The use of the verb *ʿlh* in 1 Sam 6:21; 7:1 does not derive from 2 Sam 6:2[34] but from the simple fact that Kiryath-yearim lay above Beth-shemesh in the central hill country. Note that the inhabitants of Kiryath-yearim are asked to "come down" (*yrd*, 6:21). Other verbs for the movement of the ark are used in the preceding narrative because the preceding action takes place for the most part on the Philistine plain, where *ʿlh* would be inappropriate. Moreover, Schicklberger's view that the name Eleazar originated in 2 Sam 6 is totally dependent on the unprovable and highly unlikely assumption that the writer of 1 Sam 7:1 intentionally altered *ʿzh* to *ʾlʿzr*.[35] Given our very limited evidence for Israelite prosopography, much of which is late and, to some extent, artificial, such speculation about names is worthless as a foundation for further discussion.

In our opinion, the links between 1 Sam 4–7 and 2 Sam 6 are to be explained partly by the other direction of dependency, and partly by historical memory. The author of 2 Sam 6 had the earlier narrative 1 Sam 4–7 before him, and his shaping of the later material, particularly the incident of the death of Uzzah, has been influenced by the theology of the earlier ark narrative. It is unlikely that the reference to the house of Abinadab is due to this literary influence, however; else one would expect some mention of Eleazar. Far more likely is the assumption that the house

31. See above, chapter 1.

32. *Ladeerzählungen*, 144–47.

33. Th. C. Vriezen, "De Compositie van de Samuël-Boeken," *Orientalia Neerlandica* (Oostersch Genootschap in Nederland; Leiden: Sijthoff, 1948), 180, 188.

34. Schicklberger, *Ladeerzählungen*, 145.

35. Ibid.

of Abinadab is mentioned simply because that was where the ark was at the time of David's action. Eleazar is omitted because, for one historical reason or another, he was no longer around. Uzzah and Ahyo are included because historically they were the ones involved in the event our later author is recording.

It is clear that 2 Sam 6 resumes the story of the ark, but that does not prove that these chapters were originally a single unit. Willis has demonstrated this quite effectively with two cogent analogies that are worth repeating:

> There are other cases in I–II Samuel in which the narrator drops a thread of his story in one chapter and does not pick it up again until several chapters later. Yet scholars do not isolate such passages as originally separate sources of traditions. Two examples connected with the so-called Ark Narrative may be cited. (1) With the deaths of Hophni and Phinehas, Eli, and the wife of Phinehas in 1 Samuel 4, the account of the Elide priesthood comes to an end temporarily. It is resumed in ch. 21 and dropped in ch. 23, resumed again briefly in 30:7ff., then in II Sam 8:17, and finally sprinkled through the Succession Narrative beginning at 15:24 and terminating at I Kings 2:26–27 (see further I Kings 2:35; 4:4). And yet, as far as I know, no scholar has suggested an original Elide Narrative comprising these passages. They appear to have an integral place in their present position. (2) David's transference of the ark to Jerusalem contains a tradition reflecting Michal's displeasure at the king's behavior (II Sam 6:16, 20–23), which assumes that the reader has already been introduced to Michal. She appears in I Sam 14:49; 18:17ff.; 19:11ff.; 25:44; II Sam 3:12ff. and after II Samuel 6 in the MT of 21:8. And yet, it is not contended that an originally isolated Michal source existed.[36]

Finally, one should observe that 1 Sam 7:1 makes a good ending to the narrative composed of 1 Sam 2:12–17, 22–25, 27–36; 4:1b–7:1. It began, following the introduction of the wicked priests and the prophecy of their demise, with the defeat of Israel, the death of the priests, and the captivity of the ark. If 7:1 were the conclusion, it would end with the victory of Yahweh, the return of the ark, and the sanctification of a new "keeper" of the ark. The language used of Eleazar in this verse clearly designates him as a priest, despite the general scholarly refusal to take that designation

36. *JBL* 90 (1971): 303.

seriously. *Qdš … l* is used particularly of the sanctification of a person for a priestly task (Exod 28:3, 41; 29:1, 44; 30:30; 40:13; Lev 8:30; 21:8), and *šmr* is often used of the exercise of priestly duties, particularly in the cultic expression *šmr mšmrt* (Num 1:53; 3:10; 18:3; 31:30, 47; etc.). Note especially Num 3:31, which refers to a priestly group's responsibility for the ark as *mšmrtm*, "their keeping." First Sam 7:1 uses *šmr* without *mšmrt*, but since our narrator is not P, that difference is hardly significant and should not obscure the cultic connotation of *šmr*.

However, if Eleazar is a priest who has assumed the cultic responsibilities toward the ark that were earlier discharged by Eli, Hophni, and Phinehas, one must take seriously the possibility that he is the faithful priest promised as a replacement for Eli's house in the early form of the oracle preserved in 2 Sam 2:35. It is true that 1 Kgs 2:27 interprets this oracle as a pro-Zadok prophecy, reflecting the later struggle between the rival priestly lines of Abiathar and Zadok, but that does not pose a major obstacle for our theory. Though the genealogical backgrounds of neither Abiathar nor Zadok are above dispute, Cross has made a good case for tracing Abiathar's line back through Eli to Moses and a somewhat weaker case for tracing Zadok back to Aaron.[37] Since Eleazar, son of Abinadab, cannot be fit into either of these genealogies, he has been largely ignored, but this is because Cross and others have not taken seriously the possibility of other rival priesthoods, totally unconnected with either Moses or Aaron. It is possible that the polemic against Eli's line contained in our passage originally stemmed from the new keepers of the ark in Kiryath-yearim. If so, David's transfer of the ark to Jerusalem, which brought it under the overpowering influence of Abiathar, David's long-time companion, and Zadok, of whom we know less, would probably have squeezed out any further priestly pretensions of Eleazar's kin, or at least any serious rivalry with Abiathar, and freed the early polemic for use by a quite different party, namely, the Zadokites. If the Aaronids, who once were partisans of a bull iconography,[38] could become keepers of the ark with its rival cherub iconography, they were quite capable of adapting a third party's anti-Elide polemic for their own use.

---

37. F. M. Cross, *Canaanite Myth and Hebrew Epic: Essays in the History of the Religion of Israel* (Cambridge: Harvard University Press, 1973), 207–15.

38. Ibid., 73–74.

3
EXEGESIS OF 1 SAMUEL 2:12–17, 22–25, 27–36

In this chapter and the next three, we shall lay out our detailed analysis and interpretation of the four chapters that make up our narrative. There is a wide, but not total, consensus that 1 Sam 4–6 make up a unified narrative.[1] We shall try to show the unity and interrelatedness of 1 Sam 2:12–17, 22–25, 27–36 and these subsequent chapters as we move through them. Text-critical matters will be dealt with largely where they have direct bearing on the interpretation of the narrative. We have made no attempt to resolve *all* the difficult textual problems of this narrative, but we have endeavored to make careful decisions in establishing the text where it is necessary for proper understanding.

2:12–17

Verse 12 is not an entirely adequate introduction for the following narrative, but it does not lack much. All that is required is a brief introduction of Eli and perhaps some statement about his age, explaining why his sons, Hophni and Phinehas, were now priest of Yahweh at Shilo.[2] Verse 12, then, points out that his sons, unlike Eli himself (cf. 1 Sam 8:1–3), were worthless fellows. Though priests, they did not know Yahweh. "Know" here apparently implies a personal experience of Yahweh's presence.[3]

The following verse presents some syntactical difficulties. As the verse now stands, *wmšpṭ hkhnym m't*[4] *h'm* appears to be the second object of the

1. See Campbell, *Ark Narrative*, 1–54, for a full summary of the positions of various scholars on the unity of this material. In light of his summary, there is no need to repeat that material here.

2. Cf. 1 Sam 1:3.

3. See Judg 2:10; 1 Sam 3:7 for parallel usages as well as for Hosea's understanding of the knowledge of God in terms of covenant obedience.

4. Reading *m't* instead of MT's *'t* with LXX and several manuscripts.

verb *yd'w* of verse 12. The priests knew neither Yahweh nor what was due the priests from the people. That is, verse 13 already begins spelling out the sins of the priests, which consisted, first of all, in ignoring the laws that regulated the priestly portions of the sacrifices (Lev 7:31ff.; Deut 18:3). This is heightened in verse 15 by *gm*, which introduces the even worse sin of the priests' demanding their portion before Yahweh received his. The syntax is difficult, however, since one expects an *'t* to precede *mšpṭ* if this were the meaning.[5]

This syntactical harshness may suggest, therefore, that the present construction of the section is due to Deuteronomistic editing. The Deuteronomic formulation in Deut 18:3 seems to be based on this passage and may support the popular emendation to *wzh mšpṭ hkhnym m't h'm*. In other words, the original narrative, after stating that the sons of Eli were worthless fellows who did not know Yahweh, gives some explanation of the normal and quite legitimate cultic practices at Shilo, before going on in verse 15 to spell out the way in which Hophni and Phinehas abused their office. Since these old practices were no longer in use at the time of the Deuteronomistic Historian, he, not unnaturally, misunderstood them as part of the description of the sins of the Elides, and edited the material to make that interpretation more obvious. *Kl 'yš zbḥ zbḥ* is a conditional or temporal clause resumed by the *waw* of apodosis: "Whenever anyone was offering a sacrifice, a servant of the priest would come while the meat was still boiling...." It is difficult to see how the practice described here and in verse 14 would be any more advantageous to the priests than the regulations found in Lev 7:31ff. and Deut 18:3; it appears rather to reflect an older cultic practice—prior to the codification of the priestly dues. One must question whether that codification was intended to restrict priestly greed or, just the contrary, to underline their legitimate claim to what they were often not receiving.

Whether it merely heightens the picture of verses 13–14 (present text) or stands in contrast to the normal cultic practice described there (possible earlier form of the text), verse 15 spells out just how degraded the priesthood had become. Even before Yahweh's portion had been burned on the altar, the priests would demand their portion of the sacrificial animal. If one accepts our reconstruction of the earlier form of the text,

5. Smith, ICC, 18.

however, the implications of the priests' behavior is even more clear. By asking for the meat before it had been boiled, they were breaking with the established cultic practice at Shilo. Obviously, if they took the meat raw, the older method of pot luck with the three-pronged fork would have to fall by the way.

At this point (2:16), the narrator has skillfully underscored the corruption of the priests by contrast to the pious and unselfish laity. As shocked as they may have been by this breech of traditional practice, the laity were quite willing to let the priests take their portion raw. They were even willing to give up as much of the sacrificial animal as the priests demanded—far more, it would seem, than the three-pronged fork had brought up in the past. The laity's only demand was that the priests burn Yahweh's portion before taking the portion for themselves. Even this minimal concession to the laity's piety was haughtily rejected, however, and the priests' demands were imposed by threat of force.

Thus (2:17) the sin of the young men was exceedingly great because they despised Yahweh's offering. *Hnʿrym* here apparently refers to the sons of Eli. *H'nšym* is to be omitted with 4QSam^{a} and LXX.

2:22–25

Verse 22 continues the narrative by portraying Eli's reaction. He was an old man, and it was only through the report of the people that he became aware of his sons' behavior.[6] *W't 'šr ... mwʿd* is lacking in LXX^{B} and 4QSam^{a}, so it may be a later addition to heighten the sons' sins.

Eli tries to dissuade his sons from their course by a fatherly speech, but to no avail. Cross and Skehan omit *'šr 'nky ... 'lh* from verse 23 as a dittography drawn mainly from the following verse, which they correct to *'l bny 'l tʿśw kn ky lw' twbh ḥšmʿh 'šr 'nky šmʿ mʿbrym bkm ʿm yhwh.*[7] The punch line to Eli's speech comes in verse 25a. Unfortunately, it is marred by textual uncertainties. *Wpllw 'lhym* is hardly correct, but Cross and Skehan's emendation following the LXX is also uncertain: *wpllw ʿlyw 'l yhwh.*[8] Nevertheless, it is difficult to regard God as the subject of the verb, since

6. Cf. 1 Sam 8:5.

7. F. M. Cross and P. Skehan, *Textual Notes on the New American Bible* (Paterson, N.J.: St. Anthony's Guild), 342.

8. Ibid.

pll is elsewhere used only with human subjects. Note particularly Ezek 16:52 and Ps 106:30, where humans intervene, in one fashion or another, to deflect the just anger of God. If a man sinned against another man, one could still appeal to God for forgiveness and protection.[9] If, however, one sinned against Yahweh himself, who could intercede for such a man? The sacrificial system existed, in part, as a way of reconciling sinful man to Yahweh, but when the priests despised the offering of Yahweh, they destroyed their sole link to forgiveness.

Noth regards 2:25b, *ky ḥpṣ yhwh lhmytm,* as Deuteronomistic,[10] but that is highly doubtful. One may compare the notation to the three certainly pre-Deuteronomistic passages in the court history where Yahweh's guidance of the course of events is made explicit.[11]

2:27–36

Verse 27 picks up and develops the final note in verse 25. An unnamed man of God comes to Eli with a message of Yahweh. Correct *hnglh* to *niglōh* and insert *ʿbdym* after *bmṣrym* with Cross and Skehan.[12] The reference to Yahweh appearing to Eli's ancestors in Egypt cannot be clearly linked to any pentateuchal passage. One can think of the selection of the Levites or the choice of Aaron, but 2:28 implies a narrower choice than that of a single tribe, and Aaron is not mentioned. Moreover, if the family of Aaron were what was referred to, it would seem to imply, as Smith pointed out,[13] that the writer lived before the descent of Zadok was traced to Aaron.

Verse 28 underscores the privileges granted by this choice, particularly stressing the priests' portion of the sacrificial offerings, in order to make clear the ungrateful nature of the Elides' behavior. Verse 29a comes close to poetry in its chiastic parallelism:

---

9. The background to the passage may be sought in the practice of using sanctuaries as places of refuge. Even when one had sinned grievously against another man, it was possible to appeal to God for protection and to have the case arbitrated (Num 35:9–28).

10. M. Noth, *Überlieferungsgeschichtliche Studien I: Die sammelnden und bearbeitenden Geschichtswerke im Alten Testament* (Darmstadt: Wissenschaftliche Buchgesellschaft, 1963 [photo-offset reproduction of the first edition, Halle an der Saale, 1943]), 61.

11. 2 Sam 11:27; 12:24; 17:14.

12. *Textual Notes*, 342.

13. Smith, ICC, 22.

lmh tbyt bgbḥy	Why did you gaze upon my sacrifice
wbmnḥty m'wyn[14]	And upon my offering cast a greedy eye.

Eli is held responsible for his sons' behavior, being accused of honoring them more than he did Yahweh, and of fattening them (*lhbry'm*) on the firstfruits of all the offerings of Israel, God's people. The reference to *r'šyt* points back to verse 16, where the priests insisted on taking their portion first.

Verses 30–31 introduces the punishment. As Schulz noted,[15] we should have expected Samuel to take the place of Eli's house, given the repeated contrast between him and the sons of Eli in the present shape of 1 Sam 2; the fact that this passage makes not the slightest reference to him points out that it originally had nothing to do with Samuel. Verse 32 seems to repeat verse 31 unnecessarily, and verse 33 may allude to Saul's slaughter of the priests at Nob. Whether either verse is original is uncertain. Verse 34 may be a prophecy *ex eventu* as Noth suggests[16]—this whole oracle may be—but that is hardly enough to characterize verse 34 as Deuteronomistic. Such a device could just as easily be attributed to the much earlier author of the ark narrative who, in any case, was writing after the death of the two men in question.

Verse 35, on the contrary, does sound Deuteronomistic, both in its use of *hqym* and its phrase *bnyty lw byt n'mn.*[17] There may have been an earlier substratum—the rejection of Eli and his house presupposes the choice of a priestly replacement—but that substratum cannot be confidently extracted from the present text with its Deuteronomistic and perhaps, even earlier, Zadokite editing.

14. Reading *tbyṭ* with LXX and 4QSam[a], deleting *'šr ṣwytty* with LXX, and reading *m'wn* as *m'wyn*, a poel denominative from *'yn*, "to eye greedily."

15. A. Schulz, *Die Bücher Samuel* (EHAT 8; Münster: Aschendorff, 1919), 51.

16. *Überlieferungsgeschichtliche Studien*, 61.

17. Cf. 1 Sam 7. On the question of the extent of Deuteronomistic influence in verses 27–36, see Stoebe, *Das erste Buch Samuelis*, 117–18.

4
EXEGESIS OF 1 SAMUEL 4

4:1b–11

4:1b–4

As many text critics have recognized, one should emend the text to include here the first part of the LXX, which would read: *wyhy bymym hhm wyqbṣw plštym lmlḥmh ʿl yśrʾl.*[18] The movement between 1a and 1b is clearly abrupt. Something has dropped out. We may assume a haplography by reason of homoiteleuton; the LXX *Vorlage* ended with *yśrʾl* as does MT 1a. With the addition, not only is the abruptness ended, but a reason is given for the Israelites going out against the Philistines. The verse as a whole thus provides a natural and satisfying opening and setting for a new unit.[19]

For *lqrʾt plštym,* it is proposed to read *lqrʾtm* "to meet them" in accord with the Septuagint and in light of the preceding emendation. The proposal here in no way affects the meaning of the text.

The form *hʾbn* should be read simply *ʾbn.* In verse 2, the precise meaning of *wtṭš* is unclear. It may be that "spread itself abroad" is the correct meaning. Others (e.g., Smith in the ICC, Cross and Skehan in the NAB) have suggested that one emend the text to *wattiqeš* (cf. 2 Sam 2:17), "the battle was hard."

18. For example, Driver, *Notes on the Hebrew Text of the Books of Samuel* (Oxford: Clarendon, 1890); Cross and Skehan (NAB); and Schicklberger, *Ladeerzählungen,* 25–26.

19. See Jared Judd Jackson, "The Ark Narratives: An Historical, Textual, and Form-Critical Study of I Samuel 4–6 and II Samuel 6" (Union Theological Seminary dissertation, 1962), 113–14; and Schicklberger, *Ladeerzählungen,* 25–26, for a more extended discussion of the text-critical issues.

No other major text-critical problems arise in this section. We are making no attempt to correct the many and varied names for the ark, but it is likely that the name of the ark has been expanded in these verses by the inclusion of *berît,* omitted by LXX.

This section begins the narrative with a typical opening temporal clause that leads into an account of the Philistines coming up to do battle against the Israelites. The narrative follows with a standard battle report indicating where the battle lines are drawn and the result of the battle—a defeat of the Israelites by the Philistines (cf. 1 Kgs 20:26–30; 2 Sam 18:6–8; 2 Sam 10:15–18; Judg 20:19–21; Judg 10:17). Then in verses 3–4, the story moves beyond the stereotyped battle report to tell of the return of the troops (*h'm*—the clan militia) to camp and the query of the elders: "*Why has Yahweh smitten us today before the Philistines?*" It is important to the movement and structure of the narrative that the initial theological concept here is that the defeat is Yahweh's doing. So, they decide to bring the ark into the camp, assuming that by so doing they will ensure Yahweh's coming to deliver them from the power (*kp*) of their enemies—an assumption the narrative will soon belie.

The section concludes with the important notation that Hophni and Phinehas were with the ark. What often goes unobserved here is that Hophni and Phinehas are as important as the ark. They are responsible, by their proximity to the ark, for its defeat and capture. *They* are the issue here, not the ark.

4:5–11

As has been indicated in the opening chapter, one of Schicklberger's principal literary critical conclusions is that verse 5 begins a new section whose action is slowed down and whose content is different from 4:1–4 because it deals only with the ark. The last point is true, but that does not make it a new section. It *is* simply and obviously the next stage in the narrative. The circumstantial clause *wyhy kbw'* does not introduce a new unit, as Schicklberger seems to suggest. Such clauses often occur within narratives. The clause does, as is frequently the case, introduce a new moment in the narrative; that is, with verse 5, we move to the next episode. But even this episode is clearly a part of the first stage of the story, that is, the battle of Ebenezer. (That verse 4 concludes a moment and verse 5 begins a new one within the first part of the narrative, becomes even clearer as we move through the analysis and look at the structure of the whole.)

With this verse, we encounter for the first time (and, appropriately, in association with the ark) the language and phenomena of holy war or the war of Yahweh—the shouting of the *t^erûʿâh* or war cry (Josh 6:5; Judg 7:20; 1 Sam 17:20, 52; cf. 2 Chr 20:21–22).[20] The people see the ark coming into camp and raise the war cry, confident that Yahweh will give them victory even though such assurance, which was customary in the holy wars, has not been given; indeed, Israel has already experienced defeat.

The Philistine response to the entry of the ark is spelled out in what follows, a response that is crucial for understanding what is happening in the story as a whole. The precise wording of the initial cry of the Philistines in the narrative is difficult to recover.[21] In any event, the fundamental character of the Philistine lament is clear. These verses set up the crucial conflict and climax of the story in 1 Sam 5 by describing the arrival of the ark as the coming of the Israelite god into battle—a point of view expressed both by the Israelites (4:3) and here by the Philistines (once again linking 4:1–4 and 5–9 together). The assumption is made in both parts that the coming of Yahweh will bring victory. This serves dramatically to underscore the unexpected and, therefore, all the more devastating report given laconically but clearly in verse 10: that the coming of the god did not bring victory. On the contrary, there was total defeat, "a great slaughter." The assumption, therefore, that the god who entered the

20. On the place of the ark in the early wars of Yahweh and the *t^erûʿāh*, see P. D. Miller Jr., *The Divine Warrior in Early Israel* (Cambridge: Harvard University Press, 1973; repr. Atlanta: Society of Biblical Literature, 2006), 145–60.

21. MT reads *bʾ ʾlhym ʾl hmḥnh*. LXX^B translates *outoi hoi theoi ēkasin pros autous eis ten parembolēn,* reflecting apparently a *Vorlage* that read *bʾw ʾlhym hʾlh ʾlhm ʾl hmḥnh*. The Lucianic witnesses (boc_2e_2) read *outos ho theos autōn ēkei eis tēn parembolēn,* reflecting apparently *bʾ ʾlhyhm ʾl hmḥnh*. The *ʾlhm* of the Septuagint may plausibly be restored to the MT as Wellhausen, Smith, Driver, and others have suggested. Haplography on the basis of homoiarkton is an obvious assumption here in light of the series *ʾlhm* being repeated at least three times (*bʾ ʾlh[y]m ʾlhm ʾl hmḥnh*). The principal problem in the MT is the singular verb when the following verse makes clear the Philistines conceive of a plurality of deities here. In light of the plural forms in LXX of verse 7 and the possibility that the orthography may not have had the final *u* vowel in the earliest forms of this story, one should perhaps translate, "Gods have come to them to their camp" (cf. the similar translation of Cross and Skehan in NAB).

battle has been decisively defeated is self-evident—or so it seems until one continues reading.

The point is accentuated by the two "woe" cries of the Philistines.[22] In the first case, the lament that nothing like this has happened to them before serves to emphasize the apparent upper hand gained by the Israelites in the coming of their god into the battle camp. Whether the lament is historically accurate is both questionable and irrelevant. Careful examination of the narrative makes us increasingly aware of the artfulness of the narrator in telling the story. Clearly, in the Philistine reaction, he is setting the stage for what follows. The claim that this action is unprecedented suggests how thoroughly demoralized and disadvantaged the Philistines would appear to be with Yahweh coming on the scene.

The second lament asks, "Who will deliver us from the hand/power (*yad*) of these mighty gods?" Their fear is of *the hand* of the Israelite god(s). If they are defeated, it will be by the divine *hand*(*s*). The lament seems to *expect* defeat by Yahweh's hand. Doubly shocking, therefore, is the report that the Philistines won an overwhelming victory; thus, the hand of the Israelite god(s) was incapable of saving the Israelites and defeating the Philistines—at least that is the only thing one can conclude at this point. The "hand" of Yahweh is an important thematic motif linking all of this together. Its meaning and significance will be discussed below.

Further reinforcement of the apparent power of the Israelite god(s) is the narrator's insertion, in the Philistine utterance, of a reference to Yahweh's smiting Egypt with plague (*mkh*—a smiting) and pestilence (verse 8).[23] The reference to the exodus calls to mind the coming of the divine warrior Yahweh in Israel's earliest history to deliver her and destroy her enemies. The Philistines fear that he is on the march once again. The significance of the description of Yahweh's power as finding expression in a

---

22. On the use of *'ôy* + *l* + suffix as a cry of lament in a hopeless situation, see G. Wanke, "*'ôy* and *hôy*," *ZAW* 78 (1966): 215–18.

23. Reading *ûbaddāber*: see Wellhausen, followed by Smith, Driver, Cross and Skehan (NAB), and others. The reading is a conjecture but a highly likely one in the context. Note the LXX includes the conjunctive *waw*, which does not make sense with *batmidbār*. Dahood makes the plausible suggestion that one read *b^{e}mō deber*, balancing *b^{e}kol makkeh*, *b* // *bm* being a stylistic phenomenon known from Ugarit. See Dahood, *Biblica* 45 (1964): 401–2, and for other possible examples of *b*//*bm*, idem, *Ras Shamra Parallels* (Rome: Pontifical Biblical Institute, 1972), 1:136, and *Ugaritic-Hebrew Philology* (Rome: Pontifical Biblical Institute, 1965), 27.

smiting with plague and pestilence is self-evident in light of what happens in 1 Sam 5–6, where Yahweh does indeed smite (*nkh,* 5:6, 9, 12) the Philistines with a plague (*mgph* is used in 6:4 rather than *dbr*). Here is one of the central structural and, in part, linguistic links between 1 Sam 4 and the following two chapters. At this point in the narrative, however, what the reader hears is the report, not of a *mkh* by Yahweh against the Philistines as the Philistine feared, but a *mkh gdwlh* by the Philistines against Israel (4:10)!

The MT of verse 9 is satisfactory as it stands. LXX^B omits from *plštym to wnlḥmtm,* but this is clearly an inner Greek error as most interpreters have recognized, a haplography due to homoiteleuton (*l'nšym … l'nšym*). The other principal Greek witnesses preserve the original Hebrew.

One should take note of a literary and theological move here that is somewhat related to, or a variation on, what W. L. Moran has called elsewhere the "Anti-Holy War" or "Unholy War."[24] In this case, it is a matter of the holy-war motifs of the Israelite action being countered by placing in the mouth of the Philistines the familiar call to take courage (*htḥzqw,* cf. Josh 10:25 and 2 Sam 10:12) and fight like men. While this is not precisely the formulation of the wars of Yahweh, this similar exhortation against Israel leads to their defeat, even as such an exhortation in the past spurred them on to victory.

This stage of the narrative concludes with the report that, despite the entry of the ark and, apparently, Israel's God, the Philistines inflicted a massive defeat on the Israelites. As a part of this report, two additional facts are noted: the capture of the ark and the death of Hophni and Phinehas, "the two sons of Eli." Both facts are crucial to the narrative. They point back to the beginning of the narrative, to the announcement of judgment against Hophni and Phinehas (2:25, 34), and to the report that they were with the ark (4:4). Now they are dead. Judgment has been enacted. But the ark they watched over is captured; Yahweh is apparently defeated and carried off. What will be the outcome of this? The rest of the narrative will work that out. What should have been a great victory for Israel and her god—there is nothing in the narrative apart from the references to Hophni and Phinehas to prepare one for any other result—has turned into a terrible defeat.

---

24. W. L. Moran, "The End of the Unholy War and the Anti-Exodus," *Biblica* 44 (1963): 333–42.

4:12–22

4:12–18

The second half of the chapter deals entirely with the report of the death of Hophni and Phinehas and the capture of the ark and the effects of that report, first on Eli (4:12–18), and then on Phinehas's wife (4:19–22). There are some textual problems in these verses, but a resolution of them is possible apart from the more radical textual and literary proposals of Schicklberger.[25] He is bothered by the *wybw'* introducing verse 13a with no goal or starting point named. He regards *whnh ʿly yšb ʿl hks'* as an insertion from another hand, namely, the author of 4:5–9, and the problematic *yd* (Q) *drk mṣph* as referring to the Benjaminite runner coming by way of "Mizpah." The clause *whnh ʿly yšb ʿl hks'* he then connects with 14a, which is similar in form and style to 4:6, and sees all of this as a continuation of 4:5–9.

Such literary critical fragmentation is both undesirable and unnecessary. To begin with, the excision of Eli from 4:13 leaves the *wh'š b'* at the beginning of 13b the same kind of "superfluous" repetition of subject (and verb) that bothers Schicklberger in 4:10 and leads him to see a break there. Only here he has made the repetition even more bothersome than it is there.

We would propose to read in verse 13 with LXX: *(l)yd hšʿr mṣph hdrk* (so also Wellhausen, Smith, and others) and translate along the lines of the NAB: "When he arrived, behold Eli was sitting in his chair beside the gate, watching the road, for his heart was troubled about the ark of God."

The man, however, went to make known his news in the city, "and all the city cried out." It is clear from 4:14 that Eli is waiting at another point, to which place the messenger finally comes with the news. (Textually, it may be preferable to read *wh'š mhr wyb' 'l ʿly* at the beginning of 4:16 rather than at the end of 4:14.)

The messenger reports the news that he has fled from the battle,[26] whereupon Eli asks him: *meh hāyāh haddābar bᵉnî*? Schicklberger proposes, with some plausibility, that the basic outcome of the battle is clear from the messenger's report that he fled and that Eli's question should be

25. *Ladeerzählungen*, 32ff.

26. In place of the first *hmʿrkh* in 4:16, read *hmḥnh* with the LXX.

read as a question about his sons: *meh hāyāh (had)dābar bānay?*[27] Two things stand against this proposal, however. One is the fact that, according to the narrative (4:13 and 18), Eli is just as concerned about and desirous of news of the ark as he is of his sons. This is not inconsistent with 1 Sam 2:34, for there the pending fate of the sons has been made clear. The other obstacle to Schicklberger's proposal is the fact that in 2 Sam 1:4 we have an almost identical set of circumstances: the report to David by a man from Saul's camp about the defeat of the Israelite army at the hand of the Philistines. The man first tells David he has escaped (as does the Benjaminite in 1 Sam 4), signaling the defeat. But David, as did Eli, asks him: *meh hāyāh haddābār*? It is only after the further report of the death of Saul and Jonathan that David goes on to inquire specifically about them in a second question. The analogy, therefore, would suggest that we read the MT as it is.

In verse 17, the messenger (called here a *mbśr* though that term usually refers to the bearer of *good* news, news of victory, not of defeat; this is the only clear exception) reports in detail the results of the battle. Four things have happened according to the report:

— Israel has fled.
— The people, or troops, have suffered a great slaughter.
— Eli's two sons, Hophni and Phinehas have been killed.
— The ark of God has been captured.

This report builds to a climax in that the last two items, the death of the sons and the capture of the ark, are the most important. It is upon receiving this news that Eli falls to his death. The coming into battle of the ark of God does not lead to victory but rather to divine defeat. It is the word about the ark more than the news of his sons' death that causes Eli to fall and break his neck. The fate of his sons is a foregone conclusion, one that Eli had been prepared for (2:34). What shocks him and leads to his own death is the information that not only have his sons died, but that the holy ark of God, the most sacred object of Israel's worship, is in enemy hands. This was not anticipated and was a devastating piece of news for Israel's leader.

---

27. *Ladeerzählungen*, 35–36.

Schicklberger is not inclined to see Eli's death as a divine judgment, because there is no indication that it is; natural explanations are given, and chapters 4ff. must not be assumed to have an original connection with chapters 1–3.[28] But this last argument ignores the evidence because of prior assumptions about its relevance. The destruction of the Elide house as the judgment of God is the whole point of 2:12–17, 22–25, 27–36. In this section of 1 Sam 4 (i.e. verses 12ff.), the fall of that house is also the point, together with the lament over the fate of the ark. Those two matters must be seen together to understand 1 Sam 4–6 in their context. The deaths of Hophni, Phinehas, Eli, and Phinehas's wife are not incidental or coincidental. They are the fulfillment of the divine words of 2:27–36. The chapter and the incidents it records are, therefore, expected. They fulfill the words of 2:27–36 and resolve the problem in Israel of which 2:12–17, 22–25 speak. But the resolution of one problem has created an even greater problem—the capture of the ark and throne of God. So, throughout these verses, even as the deaths of the Elides are reported, the lament over this greater tragedy is made. The way in which the deaths are reported without reference to divine judgment is appropriate in this context. How can these acts be seen as the work of God, when the consequence of the battle has been the defeat and powerlessness of Yahweh as indicated by the defeat and slaughter of the Israelite troops and the capture of the ark by the enemy? That is precisely the problem that 1 Sam 5 and 6 will work out.

Schicklberger sees the *wyhy* of 4:18 as a new introduction that separates verse 18 from the preceding verses; verse 19 is intimately connected with verse 18 by the third-person suffix on *kltw,* which, Schicklberger notes, is not understandable apart from the preceding verse.[29] But Schicklberger's literary analysis at this point ignores two things. One is, again, the frequent use of *wyhy* at the beginning of dependent clauses, particularly when in conjunction with the preposition and infinitive construct. In such cases, the *wyhy* does not necessarily form a new section. Further, the third-person suffix on *khzkyrw* (4:18), which has to refer to the messenger, connects verse 18 to verse 17 just as surely as the suffix on *kltw* connects verse 19 to verse 18. All of verses 12ff. are a section in the

28. Ibid., 36.
29. Ibid., 37.

narrative. In terms of content, verses 12–18 focus on Eli, verses 19–22 on Phinehas's wife.[30]

4:19–22

Verse 19–22 form the final unit of 1 Sam 4 and, while introducing a new element in the story, are clearly connected to and grow out of the preceding verses, both syntactically and in terms of content. The section is clear and does not pose major difficulties. Verse 22 is probably an addition meant to underscore the capture of the ark inasmuch as that becomes the focus of 5:1ff. It is a transition into 1 Sam 5 and should not be excised too easily.

Verses 19–22 deal with the reaction of Phinehas's wife to the bad news and her subsequent death. The only raison d'être the section can have grows out of the woman's relation to Eli and Phinehas. As in the report to Eli, the critical and shattering news is of the death of the Elides and the capture of the ark. Those two motifs cannot be separated here any more than in the rest of the chapter, where they are held together. Rost proposed to strike *w'l-hmyh w'yšh* from *'l-hlqh 'rwn h'lhym wmt hmyh w'yšh* in verse 19 and from the end of verse 21 on the grounds that they are additions that introduce a new thought and affect the clarity of the text.[31] Without them, the concern of the text is only about the ark. But here, as Schicklberger has recognized,[32] is where Rost lets his presuppositions about the nature and intention of the narrative control his literary and textual work. Rather than accepting the text and letting it shape his understanding of the narrative, Rost lets his assumption that the passage as a whole concerns the wandering of the ark lead him to excise elements that do not fit that impression. But these verses clearly have to do with the death of the Elides and those related to them (though we are not told of Ichabod's fate), as well as the capture of the ark. Apart from reference to the death of Eli and Phinehas, the section about the death of Phinehas's wife makes little sense. Some commentators have remarked on the peculiarity of the

30. The *bʿd yd* of verse 18 is probably not the original text. One should perhaps correct here with Wellhausen and others to read *byd*. See the discussion in J. Wellhausen, *Der Text der Bücher Samuelis* (Göttingen: Vandenhoeck & Ruprecht, 1871), 57. The last part of verse 18 is apparently a Deuteronomistic chronological convention.

31. Rost, *Thronnachfolge*, 12.

32. *Ladeerzählungen*, 37.

expression *wk't mwth* in verse 20, which seems to assume that the death of the mother was a regular occurrence at childbirth. Schicklberger has, probably correctly, discerned the reason for the expression by suggesting that the significance of the fate of the Elides for the author was such that the death of the wife of Phinehas seemed self-evident.[33]

The terrible plight of Israel and the defeat of her God is signaled by the repeated lament of Phinehas's wife that the ark has gone into exile (*glh*). Schicklberger sees in 4:19–21 an etymological tradition but assumes properly that the section has never existed without the connection to verses 11–18 and belongs to an ancient tradition according to which all three moments—loss of the ark, death of the father-in-law, and death of the husband—are of significance for the name "No glory."[34]

33. Ibid.
34. Ibid., 42.

5
EXEGESIS OF 1 SAMUEL 5

Chapter 5 is composed of two sections (5:1–5 and 6–12) that clearly hold together, cannot be separated into different literary strata or tradition complexes, and flow directly out of 1 Sam 4. Verse 1a, with its reference to the capture of the ark (*lqḥw 't 'rwn h'lhym*; cf. verses 19, 21, and 22) connects ch. 5 clearly with the preceding verses and, at the same time, shifts the scene to the Philistines as it continues the story.

Schicklberger, as we have noted earlier, has argued that 1 Sam 5 and 6 did not have an original connection with chapter 4 except for 4:5–9. In 4:5–9 he sees a theological view of the ark that is different from the rest of chapter 4 but the same as that in chapters 5 and 6. That is, the ark in these parts is surrounded by massive religious conceptions that are not present in the main part of chapter 4. Power goes forth from the ark and is attributed to it, and the ark is associated with the deity in 4:5–9 and chapters 5 and 6. But, according to Schicklberger, that is not true of the ark in the rest of 1 Sam 4. Such an argument, however, will not stand, either in terms of a valid understanding of the ark or in terms of the unity of the narrative. The observation about a different understanding of the ark is pointless. One cannot justify the neat distinction in the history of the role of the ark except possibly over a very long period of time. Furthermore, 4:3 clearly assumes the power of the ark and its association with the deity, and the rest of the chapter after verse 9 does not require mention of the powers of the ark. When we come to 1 Sam 5, it becomes important to the story once again.

Schicklberger also argues for a common terminology with reference to the ark that differs from the terminology used in 4:10–22.[1] But an analysis of the ark designations in 1 Sam 4–6 in both MT and LXX, even when

1. *Ladeerzählungen*, 88.

bryt is deleted as a Deuteronomistic addition, has to acknowledge the diversity of terminology that shows no clear pattern permitting a separation of sources according to how ark terminology appears.[2]

Schicklberger give further reasons for seeing 5:1ff. as distinct from 4:10–22: the Elides fade into the background; the Philistines are political opponents in 1 Sam 4 (which is just as true of 4:5–9) but worshipers of foreign gods in 1 Sam 5 and 6; and in chapter 5 the geographical horizon moves beyond Ephraim's tribal boundaries into the international sphere.[3] But these arguments are obviously without weight. All of the changes and differences noted by Schicklberger are attributable to the movement of the story and should not be regarded as testimony to different literary or tradition sources.

5:1–5

The placing of *plštym* at the beginning of verse 1 is not, as Campbell supposes, in order to give it emphatic position, but to break the tense sequence out of chapter 4.[4] Chapter 5 picks up with a perfect tense, indicating a new section in the narrative. The obvious similarity of verse 1 and verse 2a has led several interpreters to see a doublet here that reflects two literary sources or a supplementary process. Campbell notes the repetition of *plštym* as the subject of verse 2 rather than *'šdwdym,* which would be expected from the end of verse 1.[5] He notes that "v. 6 follows smoothly upon v. 1" and suggests quite plausibly that verses 2–5 have been inserted between 1 and 6; verse 1 now functions as "a general introduction to the events in Philistia."[6] He thus sees the unit here as 5:2–4(5) and regards 5:1 as playing its role on the level of the composition of the whole narrative. Now, while it is possible to see 5:1 as introducing the rest of the

---

2. The designations of the ark in 1 Sam 4–6 are as follows:
'rwn (h)'lhym—4:11, 13, 17, 18, 19, 21, 22; 5:1, 2, 10 (twice)
'rwn yhwh—4:6; 5:3, 4; 6:1, 2, 8, 11, 15, 18, 19, 21; 7:1
'rwn bryt yhwh—4:3, 4, 5
'rwn 'lhy yśr'l—5:7, 8 (three times), 10, 11; 6:3
h'rwn—6:13.

3. *Ladeerzählungen*, 100.

4. *Ark Narrative*, 83.

5. Ibid., 84.

6. Ibid., 84–85.

narrative and verses 2–5 as an insertion, there is a very strong reason for regarding this doublet as stylistic expansion within a single literary unit, that is, verses 1–5: verse 3 depends upon and assumes information from *both* verse 1 and verse 2. Verse 1 provides the information that the ark was brought to Ashdod, a fact that is picked up with reference to the Ashdodites in verse 3.[7] Verse 2 provides the information that the ark was set up in the temple of Dagon beside Dagon, a fact that is crucial to the rest of the section.

The LXX has a reading that must reflect *wyb'w byt dgwn wyr'w* after *mmhrt.* Wellhausen and others adopt this reading for clarity. It is possible that the LXX addition represents an original reading that dropped from the MT in the process of transmission, but it is difficult to say that with certainty. The form *lpnyw* is not what normal usage requires after *npl* in verses 3 and 4, inasmuch as *lpny 'rwn* appears immediately afterwards. Wellhausen, Driver, Stoebe, and others read *'l pny* in both cases, as, apparently, does LXX. As Campbell notes, the repetition of the form makes the emendation uncertain.[8]

In verse 4b the word *dgwn* hardly can be correct in the sentence *rq dgwn nš'r 'lyw.* It is probably to be read with most commentators as *gēwô, gēw dāgôn*, or *giz'ô.*[9]

The climax and turning point of the whole narrative of 1 Sam 4–6 is in these verses.[10] The preceding chapter has recorded an astonishing defeat that the Israelites suffered at the hands of the Philistines, one terrible consequence of which was the capture of the Israelite ark by the Philistines.

---

7. One cannot assume from the reference to *byt dgwn* that Ashdod is automatically meant. Judg 16 requires the assumption of a *byt dgwn* in Gaza, and several places mentioned in biblical and extrabiblical sources bear the name *byt dgwn.* See F. J. Montalbano, "Canaanite Dagon: Origin, Nature," *CBQ* 13 (1951): 381–97.

8. *Ark Narrative, 85*, M.2.

9. The last is the reading of Cross and Skehan in the NAB translation, citing LXX *hē rhachis dagōn* and Vulgate *Dagon truncus solus.*

10. This passage has not received the attention it merits, either with regard to its central position in 1 Sam 4–6 or as an example of the conflict between Yahweh and the gods. Among the many studies of this material, two articles that have given it some special attention are A. Bentzen, "The Cultic Use of the Story of the Ark in Samuel," *JBL* 67 (1948): 37–53; and M. Delcor, "Jahweh et Dagon," *VT* 14 (1964): 136–54. Both Schicklberger and especially Campbell have emphasized the place of this episode in the narrative, though Campbell is more perceptive than Schicklberger in recognizing the theme of the battle of the gods.

In our survey of the Near Eastern data in the first chapter, we set forth the various motivations and ideologies behind the taking and return of divine images.[11] The capture of the ark undoubtedly belongs to this framework. It was seen by the Philistines as some form of representation of the deity (see 1 Sam 4:7). One may assume that it was understood as booty, as was commonly the case. But the narrative goes beyond that, both from the perspective of the Israelites and from that of the Philistines.

From the point of view of the Israelites, the ark has been captured (*lqḥ*, verses 11, 17, 19, 21, and 22) and has gone into exile (*glh*, verses 21 and 22). Both expressions indicate that the Israelites understood this as an involuntary departure of the ark. There is no effort here to ascribe the loss of the ark to the anger of the Israelite deity, as is usually the case. The verb *glh* always involves a compelled departure under the subjugation and control of others. A comparable expression occurs in Hos 10:5, where it is said of the calf of Beth-aven that its glory (*kābôd*) has gone into exile from it. This is commonly understood as the Assyrians' taking the gold trappings of the calf as tribute. It is not a willing departure. At the same time, we note that on the occasion, when indeed the "glory" left Israel as a reflection of God's judgment on his people (Ezek 10–11), nothing is said about the glory departing Israel and *going into exile*, though that is indeed what happened.[12]

So, in 1 Sam 4, rather than having abandoned his people in anger, Yahweh, represented in the form of the ark, seems to have bowed to the superior might of the Philistine gods—an assumption that frequently lies

11. Cf. M. Cogan, *Imperialism and Religion: Assyria and Judah in the Eighth and Seventh Centuries B.C.E.* (SBLMS 19; Missoula, Mont.: SBL and Scholars Press, 1974).

12. Note also that in the "Lamentation over the Destruction of Ur" and the "Lamentation over the Destruction of Sumer and Ur" gods and goddesses are pictured as departing and abandoning in anger or by their own will. But such deities are not spoken of as going into exile. Cf. characteristic examples of the divine abandonment from the annals of Sennacherib cited by Cogan, *Imperialism and Religion*, 11:

ilānīšum īsibūšunūtima
Their gods abandoned them
ša īsibūšu ilānīšu
… whom his gods had abandoned.

(Both texts are found in D. D. Luckenbill, *The Annals of Sennacherib* [OIP 2; Chicago: University of Chicago Press, 1924], 64 and 61.)

behind the taking away and spoliation of divine images, though it is usually the perspective of the conqueror rather than the conquered.[13]

When one turns, in order to determine the Philistine view of the event, to the account in the narrative of what the Philistines did with the ark, one finds a brief report in 5:12 that the captured ark was carried to one of the principal Philistine cities, Ashdod, and set up (*yṣg* hiphil) in the house of Dagon (*byt dgwn*) alongside (*'ṣl*) Dagon. The house of Dagon is clearly the temple of Dagon, the chief Philistine deity. We know from Assyrian sources that the statues of the gods were treated as booty. But surely there is more than that involved here. Middle Assyrian texts from the reign of Tiglath-pileser I (roughly contemporaneous with the time of the battle of Ebenezer) indicate that the Assyrian rulers sometimes presented the captured gods to their own gods.[14] The captured gods were also honored by the Assyrians because they abandoned their own people to recognize the might and power of Ashur by coming to praise and honor him.[15] Cogan suggests that Amaziah's act of setting up the gods of the Edomites and worshiping them (2 Chr 25:14) reflects this practice.[16] It is also likely that the Philistine handling of the ark is a similar step. It is set up, suggesting it functioned in some sense as a divine image and an object of worship. Also, it is alongside (*'ṣl*) Dagon, indicating its place as an object of worship and as a captured god honoring the might of Dagon. The Philistines could render homage to Yahweh, who, from their perspective, would be seen as having abandoned his people to acknowledge the power and superiority of Dagon.

Such an interpretation of the Philistine act is consistent with their earlier reaction to the entry of the ark into battle. Then they had seen that event as a threatening one because the god(s) of the Israelites had entered the conflict on their side. The subsequent surprising victory of the Philistines would seem to be a testimony to two things: the superiority of Dagon (implicit in the Israelite reaction) and the abandonment by Yahweh of his

13. Cogan, *Imperialism and Religion*, 40. "[Neo-Assyrian] spoliation of divine images was meant to portray the abandonment of the enemy by his own gods in submission to the superior might of Assyria's god, Ashur." For specific examples, see the Esarhaddon inscriptions quoted by Cogan, 35 and 37 (also in *ANET*, 291).

14. Cogan, *Imperialism and Religion*, 27.

15. Ibid., 20.

16. Ibid., 116–17.

people in recognition of that superiority (implicit in the Philistine reaction but not in the Israelite).

It is at this place in the narrative, beginning with 5:3, that we have the turning point. Even as the outcome of the encounter of the armies had been something of a surprise, so now the encounter of the gods turns out to be a surprise also. In that event is the beginning of the resolution of the whole affair—indeed, it is the vindication of Yahweh. The rest of the narrative flows out of this astonishing and somewhat enigmatic encounter, a conflict that can only be understood in terms of the battle of the gods. The battle is portrayed in subtle and indirect ways rather than directly, but we are able to understand it more clearly in light of the mythological texts from Ugarit.[17]

The crucial clause is repeated twice (5:3 and 4), with an important elaboration the second time. In the MT it is as follows: *whnh dgwn npl lpnyw 'rṣh lpny 'rwn yhwh.* The preposition *lpnyw* has been the subject of much discussion. Delcor would see the suffix as referring to Yahweh. This is a possibility and, indeed, one that is very much in accord with the approach to the passage in these paragraphs.[18] But the context of the preceding verses would indicate the ark as the antecedent of the suffix, in which case we have a redundancy that is rather unusual.[19] Most commentators have agreed with Wellhausen and Driver here in emending the text to read *npl ʿl pnyw,* which seems to be the Hebrew behind the LXX's *epi prosōpon autou.*[20] While the emendation is by no means certain, we consider that it has a high degree of probability.

---

17. In his dissertation, Campbell (*Ark Narrative*, 86 n. 1) has a brief note in which he refers to one of the Ugaritic texts discussed in the following pages. But Campbell makes no attempt to develop the parallel as background for the Yahweh-Dagon encounter. In his dissertation (1963) published in revised form in 1973, Miller signaled the importance of this Ugaritic material for understanding 1 Sam 5:1–5 and gave a brief but basic interpretation of the encounter. (See P. D. Miller Jr., *The Divine Warrior in Early Israel* [Cambridge: Harvard University Press, 1973; repr., Atlanta: Society of Biblical Literature, 2006], 253–54 n. 246). That interpretation was elaborated in a paper entitled "Yahweh Versus Dagon: An Analysis of I Samuel 5:1–5 in Its Context," read before the Colloquium for Old Testament Research, 23–25 August 1973.

18. M. Delcor, "Jahweh et Dagon," *VT* 14 (1964): 148.

19. See the discussion of the problem of a redundancy or explanatory addition in S. R. Driver, *Notes on the Hebrew Text of the Books of Samuel* (Oxford: Clarendon, 1890), 50.

20. The LXX phrase could be a translation of *l'appāyw,* but it is highly unlikely that it represents *l*ᵉ*pānāyw.*

There are two possible interpretations for this clause in verse 3. One is the perfectly plausible interpretation of Dagon's prostration as an act of worship. This may well be the correct view of the happening described in verse 3. The ark has been set up in homage to Dagon and as an object of worship. The act clearly indicates the intended—the superiority of Yahweh. The tables are turned. Rather than Yahweh doing homage before the mightier Dagon, it is Dagon who prostrates himself before Yahweh. Certainly the idiom here is fairly common in this sense (*npl* [*'l-pny*] *'l-pny 'rṣh* Josh 5:14, 7:6 [before the ark]; Ezek 43:3; 44:4; Gen 17:3; Ezek 3:23; etc.).

There is an alternative interpretation with the idiom used in another sense, though not as frequently or quite as precisely. In 1 Sam 17:49 when David hits Goliath with the stone, the narrative reports *wypl 'l-pnyw 'rṣh*. In other words, the expression in Hebrew can refer to one being felled in combat—specifically, in this case, individual combat. We note further that in verse 4, a mere act of worship can hardly be meant. The cut-off hands and head of Dagon suggest a fatal fall in combat—like that of Goliath.

With this biblical parallel in mind, it is helpful to turn to the mythological texts from Ugarit, where we have some related expressions. At the end of UT 127 (CTA 16.6.54–57):

ytbr (55) *hrn . ybn.*
ytbr.hrn (56) *r'išk* [.].
'ttrt.šm.b'l (57) *qdqdk.*
tqln.bgbl

May Horon break, O my son,
May Horon break your head
Aṯtart, name of Baal, your pate,
May you fall in....

There is a parallel passage in UT 137:9 (CTA 2.1.9) which has, in place of *tqln*, the form *tpln*, one of the several instances indicating that *npl* and *ql* are synonymous and interchangeable. That interchange is exemplified in Text 68 (CTA 2.6.23–26), an important parallel to our 1 Samuel text. In that text, Baal and Yamm engage in battle and the issue is who shall rule, Baal or Yamm. In the lines referred to above, Baal strikes Yamm to the ground and "Yamm falls to the ground" (*wyql l'arṣ* 11.23 and 25–26). That is essentially what we have in 1 Sam 5:3, but with the synonym *npl*. Thus, in one of the classic divine battles, the same kind of expression appears as the one in 1 Sam 5:3.

In similar fashion, UT 67:VI:8–9 (CTA 5.6.8–9) reports the death of Baal, presumably at the hands of Mot, whom he later defeats:

> *mǵny bʿl npl lʾarṣ*
> We came upon Baal, *fallen to earth.*

The parallels are even more apropos when one turns to 1 Sam 5:4. In this second battle, Dagon falls to earth before the ark of Yahweh, that is, before Yahweh, with head and hands cut off. Here again we have, without doubt, the divine battle. Dagon falls to earth, slaughtered by Yahweh. His head and hands are cut off, a mutilation motif now known to us from Ugaritic mythology in connection with Anat. In the enigmatic *ʿnt* text (UT *ʿnt* = CTA3), there is an account of Anat's bloody battle with the "people of the west" and the "men of the east," with unnamed soldiers and warriors who appear to be human (*adm, lim, mhr, ǵzr, ṣbu*). No one, to my knowledge, has satisfactorily explained this passage. Its context does not really help us know who these fighters are who attack Anat and what part this plays in the Baal-Anat cycle. Cassuto has suggested that: "Apparently these were human beings who belonged to Baal's opponents."[21] Virolleaud saw here the allies of Mot.[22] That may not be as unusual as it seems at first. The allying of human and divine armies is a fairly common motif in the Old Testament.[23] So Anat may well be fighting the allies of Mot, and it is another instance of the divine conflict.

The particular thing to note is that in the battle, Anat cuts her enemies in pieces (*tḥtṣb*); the same terminology is used for Yahweh's slaughter of Rahab in Isa 51:9ff. What this means is spelled out more explicitly in the Ugaritic text, where it says that heads (*rʾš*) and palms of hands (*kp*) are under her and she hangs heads on her back and palms on her girdle. This is less common than it may seem. M. Pope has pointed out a very

---

21. U. Cassuto, *The Goddess Anath* (trans. I. Abrahams; Jerusalem: Magnes), 87.

22. C. Virolleaud, *La déese ʿAnat* (MRS 5; Paris: Geuthner, 1938), 11.

23. Meroz is cursed for not coming to the help of Yahweh with/among the warriors in Judg 5:23. See P. D. Miller Jr., *The Divine Warrior in Early Israel.*

strong parallel with the Indian goddess Kali.[24] There are other analogues, particularly Hathor (Sekhmet) in the Egyptian account of the salvation of humanity, but there it is simply the gory goddess, to use Pope's apt phrase, not the explicit cutting off of palms of hands and heads.

Needless to say, this is exactly the state of affairs when the Ashdodites find Dagon the second time. Not only is he fallen to earth again, but his head and the palms of his hands are cut off. In both cases, it is *kp yd* and not just *yd* that are cut off. The battle is over. Yahweh has not only felled Dagon, but he has hewn or cut him in pieces even as in mythopoeic language he cut Rahab in pieces (Isa 51). Thus, the ancient mythological motif of the battle of the gods, which is present in various fragments in the Old Testament (Isa 51; Pss 74 and 89; Isa 27), appears here at the center of a historical narrative in a nonmythological context and forms the climax of that narrative. The superiority of Yahweh in the divine realm has been established first. The Philistine victory did not mean, as one might have supposed (Israelite or Philistine), that Dagon was mightier than Yahweh or Yahweh subject to Dagon. On the contrary, Yahweh rules in the divine world. And, as the next section will manifest, that rule extends to and has implications for the human sphere also.

The conclusion of this episode is found in the etiological note in verse 5, which is clearly secondary. The point is quite irrelevant to the context. It is a familiar kind of etiology—the explanation of a primitive religious custom the origin of which is no longer known. It has been added here because of the reference to threshold in verse 4.[25] At the same time, the etiology does serve to give verisimilitude to the story.

---

24. M. Pope, *Wörterbuch der Mythologie* (ed. H. W. Haussig; Stuttgart: Klett, 1962), 1.1:239.

25. B. S. Childs, "A Study of the Formula 'Until This Day,'" *JBL* 82 (1963), 287–88: "1 Sam 5:5 has retained a pure etiological form, yet again a dislocation in content has occurred. Vs. 5 establishes etiologically an ancient cultic practice: 'the priests of Dagon do not tread on the threshold until this day.' Numerous parallels from comparative religion reveal that this is a mark of special reverence. Yet the actual story which provides the etiology recounts the humiliation of Dagon and forms part of the ark tradition. We infer that in the present story the original Canaanite cult etiology has been mutilated and all except the final sentence has been replaced by Hebrew tradition. The highly incongruous effect of the fusion appears to be a conscious device of the author, perhaps for the purpose of ridicule. Again, the evidence is unequivocal that the tradition in verses 1–4 was independent of the etiological formulation."

5:6–12

The text of 1 Sam 5:6–12 appears to be quite corrupt. A comparison of MT, 4QSam[a], the LXX, and the other versions suggests all our extant texts are defective. At least two verses appear to have fallen out or been conflated with other verses in the section. The summary statement in 6:17 suggests the ark visited each of the major cities of the Philistine pentapolis during its seven-month sojourn in Philistine territory (6:1). It is possible that 6:17 is a secondary expansion, but the verse as it stands would explain the textual confusion in 5:10 between Ekron and Ashkelon. The verses dealing with the two cities were conflated, but the city name preserved in the conflate text differed in the textual traditions. The verse dealing with Gaza, on the contrary, has simply been lost, and it is impossible to be sure of the original order, though the order in 6:17 is suggestive.

A number of textual problems that are probably not capable of full resolution appear in verse 6. Driver and Stoebe, among others, give fairly full discussion of these. The word *way^{e}šimmēm* is not entirely clear. It does not normally mean "ravage" or "lay waste" persons, and the alternate meaning ("horrify, appall") seems rather weak in the context.[26] A number of interpreters[27] have followed Ehrlich in hypothesizing an error in one consonant and reading *way^{e}hummēm,* a reading they find supported by Aquila's *eqhagedainisen,* a verb that Aquila uses elsewhere to translate *hāmam.* In light of the use of this verb elsewhere in this unit, the suggestion is quite plausible. However, in light of LXX, it may be that the original text read *wayyohom 'et ha ašdôdîm.*[28]

The LXX preserves a fuller text tradition in this verse. It is reflected in Cross and Skehan's translation in the NAB, where they assume in the original text after *g^{e}bûleyha* the following: *wayya'al '^{a}lêhem 'akbarîm '^{a}šer šar^{e}ṣû bo'^{o}niyyōtām wayya'^{a}lû b^{e}tôk 'arsām watt^{e}hî m^{e}hûmat māwet gedôlā bā'îr.* Their translation of the whole verse is as follows: "He ravaged and

26. It is not supported by B's *epēgagen, contra* Stoebe, because far from being the translation of *wyšmm* misread as *way^{e}šîmēm, epēgagen autois* is only a mutilated fragment of the more complete line *epēgagen autois muas* (bh) or *epēgagen ep autous muas* ($dopzc_2e_2$).

27. E.g., Driver and Schicklberger. Cf. Willis, *JBL* 90 (1971), 295 n. 35.

28. Reading with $bdhopc_2e_2$. If the emendation is correct, *wayyohom* would also point back to 4:5. There the earth shook at the Israelites' shout; here Yahweh strikes the Ashdodites with panic.

afflicted the city and its vicinity with hemorrhoids; he brought upon the city a great and deadly plague of mice that swarmed in their ships and overran their fields."

When we turn to the literary character of the passage and its interpretation, it is immediately clear that the narrative moves out of the climactic engagement with Dagon to further demonstrate Yahweh's power over the Philistines and their god (5:7) as the ark is carried throughout the Philistine pentapolis. In each place it is said that the "hand of Yahweh" was against that city, the same "hand" that was feared at Ebenezer (4:8) but *seemed* to have been ineffective. The hand of Yahweh/Elohim being heavy against the Philistines is the unifying theme of this section and, indeed, is a fundamental and unifying theme for the whole narrative. In this section, it forms an *inclusio* (verses 6 and 11) of sorts and appears also in verses 7 and 9.

In a brief article in 1971, Roberts examined the expression "the hand of Yahweh/Elohim" in the light of similar expressions in extrabiblical materials.[29] There it was shown that virtually all the formulations in this narrative are paralleled in Akkadian sources.[30] Furthermore, the expression is not derived from the exodus, as Zimmerli suggested earlier, but is common Near Eastern language for speaking about plague and pestilence, which are seen as coming from the deity. Even in the exodus itself, one can see the relationship between the hand of Yahweh and plague (Exod 9:3). At the same time, one notes in the context immediately before us explicit use of the hand of Yahweh motif along with allusions to the exodus. Both the association with plague and the character of the hand of God as a disastrous manifestation of the power of Yahweh in the exodus occur in 4:8, where the hand of God is feared because it brought plague and pestilence in the exodus. In 6:6, allusion is also made to the exodus in the context of an admonition to the Philistines not to harden their hearts as did the Egyptians and Pharaoh, so that perhaps Yahweh will lighten "his hand" from off them and their gods.

---

29. J. J. M. Roberts, "The Hand of Yahweh," *VT* 21 (1971), 244–52.

30. *watt*^{e}*hî yad-yhwh bā'îr* (1 Sam 5:9) // *qāti Rašap ibašši ina mātīya*; *yādō nāg*^{e}*'āh bānû* (1 Sam 6:9) // *qāti Rašap … iduk*; *tikbad yad yhwh* (1 Sam 5:6) // *kabtat qāssu*; *qāš*^{e}*tāh yādô 'ālênû* (1 Sam 5:7) // *qat Ištara-danna elīya dannat*; *yāqēl 'et-yādô mē*^{a}*lêkem* (1 Sam 6:5) // *lišaqqil qassu*; *lô tasûr yādô mikkem* (1 Sam 6:30) // *lišaqqil qassu.*

This dual association of the hand of Yahweh with plagues and with the exodus is not surprising in this context, because the motif is clearly a reflection of the divine warfare and is part of the imagery of the divine warrior. The God who fought for Israel against the Egyptians fights now against the Philistines and their gods. The cutting off of the hands of Dagon *kpwt ydyw* assumes, therefore, a larger role, for it is a manifestation of the superior power (*yad*) of Yahweh. The story as a whole conceives of the power of God and the gods entirely by means of the motif of the divine hand (4:8; 5:4, 6, 7, 9, 11; 6:3, 5, 9), which, in line with the usage of the motif in extrabiblical contexts, is manifest in the phenomena of plague.

The notion that Yahweh the warrior fights with the tools of plague and pestilence is not an idea confined to this narrative and exodus references, or even just to places where the hand of Yahweh/God plays a role. The concept is found in other forms. The march of the divine warrior in Hab 3 depicts Yahweh accompanied by plague and pestilence in his battle march (3:5). In Jer 21:5–6, the divine warrior is depicted as fighting (*nlḥmty*) "with outstretched hand and strong arm" and, as the text goes on to say, "with anger and rage and great wrath. And I will smite the inhabitants of this city, man and beast: in a great plague they will die."

Thus we encounter at the heart of the narrative a primary image that binds all of its parts together—the defeat of Israel, the defeat of Dagon, and the defeat of the Philistines—and serves to demonstrate that the power of the divine warrior Yahweh is the key to what the narrative is really about. The might of Yahweh, manifest through his hand (which works to destroy the enemy through the direct engagement in battle [Dagon] and through the indirect means of sickness and pestilence), is the thread that runs through the narrative, holding it together and conveying its intention.

The heavy hand of Yahweh and the panic of the Ashdodites is explicated in the narrative of the plague that follows. Although the meaning of *ʿplym* is disputed, it probably refers to buboes, the inflamed swelling of the lymph glands especially in the armpit or groin, that are characteristic of bubonic plague. Both Ashdod and its surrounding territory were afflicted by these buboes, which would appear to have been spread by the rodents mentioned in the next phrases. The word *ʿkbrym* is a general term that would include both mice and rats. Rodent plagues are often characterized by the rapid increase in the population of both classes of rodents. Such was the case, for instance, in the terrible west Texas plague of 1959. Both vermin became so numerous during the spring and summer of that year that quite sober eyewitness accounts sound like Texas tales. In the biblical account, the rapid expansion of the rodent population apparently began by the sea, among the Ashdodites' boats, and quickly spread to the interior. That again could point to bubonic plague, since the infected rats could have been brought in by sea from outside the Philistine territory. As a result of the population explosion of the rodents and the plague that it spread, there was a great panic in the city. *Mwt* in the reconstructed expression *mhwmt mwt gdwlh* (LXX) is to be taken as syntactically parallel to *yhwh* in the related expression *mhwmt yhwh rbh* (Zech 14:13). It is not a "deadly panic" but a "panic caused by death." What is meant is the disruption of normal social intercourse caused by the terrifying prospect of contracting the deadly disease.

Verse 7 reiterates the theme of the heavy hand of the god of Israel against both the people and their god Dagon.[31] The reaction of the Philistines to the turn of events resembles their reaction to the news of the ark's appearance in the Israelite camp in 4:7. The word *wyr'w* is normally derived from *r'h*, and *kî* is translated as "that" after the verb of seeing. Despite Ehrlich's objection, such a construction does not appear "unhebraisch," as Job 9:2 demonstrates (*yd'ty ky kn* "I know that it is so"). Nevertheless, the letters *wyr'w* could be analyzed as a form of *yr'*, precisely as they are in 4:7.[32] Then the parallel would be even closer: "The men of Ashdod feared because of what had transpired, so they said…." The remarkable temporal coincidence in the arrival of the ark, the collapse of Dagon's statue, and the outbreak of the plague is enough to move the Philistines to draw a causal connection. Thus the Ashdodites conclude that the ark of the god of Israel—a designation quite appropriate in the mouth of the Philistines—can no longer abide with them. This god had made his hand harsh (*qašah* is an unexceptional synonym to *kābēd*; see the related Akkadian pair *danānu* and *kabādu*) on them and their god Dagon. The reference to Dagon ties the account back to 5:1–5, but it was

31. The perfect *we'āmerû* may be correct, indicating action simultaneous with the preceding verb. The context, however, suggests a sequence of actions and that the verb should be emended to the imperfect with *waw* consecutive.

32. The interchange of *yr'* and *r'h* in a form such as this one is quite easy. Even in the MT the only difference would be a *metheg*. Cf. the similar uncertainty about which of these two roots is present in Gen 50:15, where the same form occurs.

the plague that drove home the implications of what had happened to Dagon's statue.

Verse 8 connects directly to verse 7 in the text as it has been preserved,[33] but if the text originally had verses dealing with Gaza and Ashkelon, one would be tempted to place them here, based on the order given in 6:17. The subject in verse 8 would then be the citizens of the last town mentioned in the material that has dropped out of the text, presumably Ashkelon. In any event, the Ashdodites, in fear before the effect of the ark, call a gathering of all the lords (*srnym*) of the Philistines to decide what to do. At this point the narrative moves very rapidly, and the economy of the writer increases the danger that critics will draw overly sharp distinctions from the narrator's choice of words. The author does not explain, for instance, how the Gittites could volunteer to receive the ark. Did they volunteer through the *seren* after agreeing to this action prior to the meeting, or was further consultation necessary after this meeting? Such details did not interest our writer. He only wanted to emphasize the Gittites' willingness to take the ark. This suggests that the spirit of the Philistines was not yet broken and that the Philistine pride was not limited to their rulers. The Gittite offer was accepted, and the ark was transferred to Gath. The movement of the ark that begins here in the narrative is not in itself the point. Rather, the shift from place to place throughout the Philistine pentapolis is a demonstration of the power of Yahweh over all the Philistines. From verse 8 on, it is clear that the scene of action is the whole of Philistia.[34]

With verse 9 a subepisode in this scene begins, as indicated by the *wyhy 'ḥry*. After the transfer, the hand of Yahweh comes upon the city, resulting in an exceedingly great panic. The expression *mhwmt gdwlh m'wd* is an appositional expression further defining what is meant by *yd yhwh*, just as *dbr kbd m'wd* in Exod 9:3.

---

33. We reconstruct the verse as follows in light of LXX and 4QSam^{a}: *wayyō'm*^{e}*rû haggittîm yassēbbû 'et '*^{a}*rôn '*^{e}*lōhê yiśrā'ēl 'ēlênû wayyassēbbû 'et '*^{a}*rôn '*^{e}*lōhê yiśrā'ēl gattāh*. If such a reconstruction is correct, it means that the move to Gath was seen as an arrogant assumption on the part of the Gittites that they could handle the ark, that no harm would come to them. Such a reading of the text suggests a stylistic or literary heightening of the action of the narrative that has its corollary in the way in which the judgment on the Gittites is described in the next verses.

34. That is true whether or not one assumes an original reference to the two other Philistine cities as places visited by the ark.

Stylistically, the account of the movement of the ark through the Philistine pentapolis reaches its climax in verses 10ff. Verse 10 records tersely that the Gittites passed the ark on to Ekron, but this time there was neither passive (5:8 MT) nor arrogant (5:8 LXX) acceptance of the ark by the citizens. Rather, they protest vigorously that this instrument of the god of Israel will bring death to them.[35] They call again the Philistine lords and protest that what has happened must be brought to an end and the ark returned to its proper place. This stage of the narrative then comes to its conclusion with an extended statement of the devastating effects of the hand of God, which has brought a panic of death—even as in the wars of Yahweh he sent panic among the enemy to defeat them—on the whole city, so that even the ones still living cry out to heaven (and implicitly either to their god, who is dead, or to Yahweh) for relief from the terrible plague.

With the response of the Ekronites and the description of their plight, it is clear that the Philistines have been defeated by the hand of Yahweh. The rest of the narrative is to show how the Philistine people managed to get out from under Yahweh's power and wrath, a state that only becomes possible after that power has been fully demonstrated and their defeat clear.

---

35. Though the singular first-person suffixes following the plural antecedent in verse 9 and the following verses are troublesome, they should probably be taken as examples of the collective "I," either as the personification of the city or as the words of the city's *seren*.

6
EXEGESIS OF 1 SAMUEL 6

6:1–9

Verse 1 marks a break. The narrative now begins to describe the actual return of the ark as a way of averting further encounter with the wrath of the god of Israel. The chronological note of verse 1 is clearly a dividing mark, indicating a transition from chapter 5 and the beginning of a new episode. (Note the use of *wyhy* at the beginning of the verse.)

The first section of chapter 6 recounts the consultation by the Philistines with priests and diviners to determine what to do with the ark. Two questions are asked in verse 2: What to do with the ark, and what to send back with it? The latter question assumes the answer to the former, and it is really with the latter question that the consultation deals, although, as Campbell suggests, verses 3ff. may be seen as the answer to the second question, while verses 7ff. may be seen as the answer to the first question.

The diviners answer the query in language typical of such officials. Assuming a certain situation exists or a certain course of action has been decided on, they point out how it should be carried through. The ark is by no means to be returned empty; they must return a compensatory offering to the God of Israel and then the Philistines will be healed. After *trp'w*, however, the MT suddenly sounds a discordant note. A check on any of the standard English translations will reveal the problem. Note the rendering of the Confraternity of Christian Doctrine version (NAB):

> They replied: "If you intend to send away the ark of the God of Israel, you must not send it alone, but must, by all means, make amends to him through a guilt offering. Then you will be healed, and will learn why he continues to afflict you."

This translation is grammatically impeccable, but the second of the two coordinated clauses, "and will learn why he continues to afflict you," does not make sense in its context. The Philistines had already surmised the reason for the plague. Moreover, once they were healed, such knowledge would be irrelevant.

Something is obviously wrong in the verse, but the popular expedient of literary-critical surgery is too radical a cure. The LXX, apparently following a Hebrew text like 4QS[a], which has *ʾz trʾp[w w]nkpr [lkm]*, reads "and then you will be healed, and he will be reconciled to you. Shall not his hand depart from you?" Thenius opted for this reading and called attention to the similar use of *nikkappēr* in Deut 21:8,[1] and Cross, in a private correspondence, also adopts this reading as original. One cannot rule out the possibility that this is correct. Nevertheless, it is difficult to see how the present MT could derive from a corruption of such a reading, while the difficulty in the MT invites corruption that could result in such a variant. Winton Thomas has attempted to resolve the problem while preserving the MT. He derives *nôdaʿ* from a second root *ydʿ*, cognate with Arabic *wadaʿa*, "to be still, quiet, at rest."[2] Under this assumption the text would make sense as it stands, while the confusion between *ydʿ* (1) and (2) would also explain the variation in the versions. Against it, however, one may raise the very serious doubt of whether the LXX translator recognized his assumed *ydʿ*.

Another solution appears more attractive to us. To begin with, one should compare this text with the plague prayers of Mursilis,[3] where the Hittites faced a problem very similar to that confronted by the Philistines in our text. A plague had raged unabated in the Hittite country for some time, and Mursilis had devoted himself to finding the reason for this expression of divine wrath. Such knowledge was important, because until one discovered why the gods were angry, one was not able to make the appropriate propitiatory offerings. Eventually Mursilis established through oracles that the plague had been sent because of two offenses: the Hittites had broken a treaty with Egypt and had neglected the offerings to the river Mala. Mursilis promises to make the appropriate restitution, but then, in his appeal for deliverance, he adds the following:

1. O. Thenius, *Die Bücher Samuels* (KeH 4; Leipzig: Hirzel, 1864), 24–25.
2. W. Thomas , "A Note on וְנוֹדַע לָכֶם in I Samuel VI, 3," JTS 11 (1960), 52.
3. See Goetze's English translation in *ANET* (1955^2), 394–96.

> But, if ye demand from me additional restitution, tell me of it in a dream and I will give it to you.
>
> See! I am praying to thee, Hattian Storm-god, my lord. So save my life! If indeed it is for those reasons which I have mentioned that people are dying,—as soon as I set them right, let those that are still able to give sacrificial loaves and libations die no longer! If, on the other hand, people are dying for some other reason, either let me see it in a dream, or let it be found out by an oracle, or let a prophet declare it, or let all the priests find out by incubation whatever I suggest to them. Hattian Storm-god, my lord, save my life! Let the gods, my lords, prove their divine power! Let someone see it in a dream! For whatever reason people are dying, let that be found out![4]

Note that Mursilis expects, or at least hopes for, deliverance as soon as he makes the restitution indicated by his oracle priests, but if the gods demand further restitution before removing the plague, or if there are other reasons for the gods' anger, the gods should at least make this known to Mursilis.

When one looks at 1 Sam 6:3 with this Hittite passage in mind, the locus of the problem shifts. The difficulty is in the simple coordination of *wnwd*ʿ and *trp'w*. The problem would disappear if one could translate the clauses disjunctively: "Then you will be healed, or else it will be made known to you why he continues to afflict you." That is, this restitution will produce the desired result, or if Yahweh has other demands, it will at least make him willing to inform you of those additional demands. Such a translation would put the passage completely in line with the theology in the comparable Hittite text and remove any need for excising the verse. It would require the assumption that an *'w*, "or," has dropped out by haplography following the *'w* at the end of *trp'w*. One would have expected the following verb to be in the imperfect, but perhaps one could explain the perfect as a secondary correction occasioned by a first mistake involving only the loss of the *aleph,* that is, an original *'z trp'w 'w ywd*ʿ became *'z trp'w wywd*ʿ, which was then corrected or misread producing the present form of the text. The Philistines then ask what kind of compensation they should return to Israel's God (6:4ff.). In verse 4 we omit *whmšy* ʿ*kbry zhb* with LXX and 4QSam[a]. This is a secondary insert based on 6:5, but in hopeless conflict with 6:18. The story originally had five buboes and

4. Ibid., 396.

an indefinite number of rats.[5] One should also read *l^{e}kull^{e}kem* instead of *l^{e}kullām*. The versions indicate both *lākem* and *l^{e}kull^{e}kem* as variants.

The response to the query is twofold: five golden buboes to recall the plague common to *seren* and commoner alike and golden rats to recall the rodents that devastated the country were to be made and presented to the god of Israel as compensation. The Philistines were also to give glory to the God of Israel.

We know of no exact ancient parallel to the Philistine procedure at this point, but the Hittite ritual against pestilence is similar enough to be suggestive.[6] It shows, first of all, that a plague could be attributed to an enemy god. A ram is given to the enemy god to pacify him, and that ram is driven toward the enemy country belonging to that god rather than being sacrificed in Hittite territory. One should also note the procedure followed in the Atrahasis epic when plague was destroying humankind.[7] The people ceased worshiping their own gods and goddesses and showered all their attention on Namtara, the god of plague. As a result, Namtara became embarrassed and "lifted his hand."

These verses do serve to make clear that, whatever conclusion one reaches about whether or not the text also originally included a report of the ark being carried to Gaza and Ashkelon, the narrative views the plague as having come upon all of Philistia. The number "five" clearly refers to the Philistine pentapolis, and verse 4 suggests that the plague covered all of Philistia (cf. 6:17–18).

The same is apparent from verse 5, which gives the theological rationale for the offering of the images. By this action, the Philistines will glorify the God of Israel and avert the *hand* of that God from the people *and their gods*, as well as their land. The narrative thus follows directly out of the earlier scenes where the hand of Yahweh has been prominent and the initial conflict has been with the Philistine god(s) (5:1–5).

The exodus typology of the narrative is picked up once more in verse 6.[8] The narrator places on the lips of the Philistine priests and diviners a

---

5. For a different view, see the general discussion of the mouse images and mouse plagues in the excursus by Schicklberger, *Ladeerzählungen*, 108–17.

6. See Goetze's translation in *ANET* (1955^{2}), 347.

7. W. G. Lambert and A. R. Millard, *Atra-hasīs: The Babylonian Story of the Flood* (Oxford: Clarendon, 1969), 66–71, 360–412.

8. For a brief discussion of this aspect of the passage, see Campbell, *Ark Narrative*, 203–4; H. J. Stoebe, *Das erste Buch Samuelis* (KzAT 8/1; Gütersloh: Mohn, 1973), 143–44.

comparison of their situation and plight to that of Egypt and Pharaoh earlier. Again Yahweh the mighty warrior has made sport (see Exod 10:1–2) of an enemy.[9] The people are warned against hardening their hearts as did the Egyptians and Pharaoh, lest they incur further the wrath of Yahweh, God of Israel.

In verses 7–9, further instructions are given, this time for how the ark shall be used to determine if the affliction suffered by the Philistines is accidental or is due to the hand of Yahweh. The focus is once more upon the power of Yahweh against his enemy. The highly alliterative verse 7 with its recurring *ayins* gives very explicit and detailed instructions on how the ark was to be returned. A new cart and untamed cows are specified because prior secular use would have profaned them and made them unfit for this mission (Num 19:2; Deut 21:3–4). Young cows with their first young calves are chosen in order to underscore the ominous nature of their behavior should they return the ark ignoring their calves, who had been penned up at home. The reference to the *kly zhb*,[10] "golden articles," that are to accompany the ark on its return provides a reflection of another exodus motif. They are to be compared with the golden articles *kly zhb* that the Israelites took from the Egyptians on their way out of Egypt.[11] Once again the wealth of the enemy goes with the Israelites—this time present in the form of the ark. The *kly zhb* are, therefore, a kind of booty or plunder that the victorious God takes on his return home.[12]

---

9. One should note that the use of *ht'll* is paralleled only in the J tradition of the exodus (Exod 10:2).

10. The use of this general noun in the plural reinforces the view that the compensatory offering consisted of objects of more than one kind.

11. Cf. Stoebe, *Das erste … Samuelis*, 147. The analogy between the two events is reinforced by the parallel between the pairing of *šlḥ* and *hlk* at the end of verse 6, referring to the departure of the Israelites, and the same pairing at the end of verse 8—this time with reference to the departure of the ark. The intentional combination of these verbs in this early narrative (see the final chapter) as a specific reference to and play on the exodus raises some questions about George Coats's treatment of Exod 3:20–21, where he sees a tension in the use of these verbs that points to a literary disjunction between the despoiling of the Egyptians' motif and its context. See G. W. Coats, "Despoiling the Egyptians," *VT* 18 (1968), 450ff.

12. Cf. Exod 3:22 and 12:36, and see the brief discussion of the intention of the despoiling of the Egyptians in B. S. Childs, *The Book of Exodus* (Philadelphia: Westminster, 1974), 177.

The reason for all these careful preparations is indicated in verse 9. The Philistines had assumed that the reason for the plague was Yahweh's anger, but without divine revelation one could not be sure. What had befallen the Philistines could have been fortuitous. Thus the Philistines take these precautions to make certain that it really was Yahweh who was responsible for the plague. On this level, their concern is obviously due to the consideration that if Yahweh was not responsible, then some other power was, and they would have to keep searching for the correct deity to appease before the plague would abate. On the narrator's level, however, the consideration would be quite different. He is attempting to undercut any skepticism his theological interpretation of history may encounter by anticipating it.[13]

13. The arguments of Rost, who is followed by others, that verses 5–9 are a secondary expansion, are unconvincing. They may be summarized as follows: (1) verse 9 reckons with the possibility of a different origin for the plague; (2) verse 6 suggests the possibility that the Philistines will change their minds and refuse to return the ark, a suggestion that would contradict the end of chapter 5 and the beginning of 6; (3) the instructions over the procedures to be followed in returning the ark show themselves to be proleptic expansion of verse 10; and (4) the speeches in these verses are longer than elsewhere in the ark narrative, where the style is terse and the speeches seldom last more than a verse. Objections 1 and 2 are too rationalistic. The positive assertion of assured facts followed by hesitant equivocation is not uncommon in contexts where the knowledge in question is derived from divination. That should be obvious from the Hittite text quoted above. Moreover, one would expect the Philistine leaders to show some reluctance about returning an object that, in their possession, had symbolized their dominance over Israel. It was only when no city would accept it, when the pressure from the people became too great, that the decision to return it was made; in this context, it is not out of place to warn against failure to carry through with the plan. The narrator's familiarity with the story of the exodus already reflected in 4:8 would make the introduction of such an eventuality unexceptionable. Objection 3 ignores the tendency of epic style to relate the giving of a command and then to narrate, often in a somewhat more abbreviated style, its execution. Finally, in answer to objection 4, the more extended, circumstantial style of verses 5–9 is better explained by the theological centrality of this passage than by its later insertion. It was theologically important to make it absolutely clear that Yahweh was responsible for all the bad things that happened to the Philistines. Only then could the narrative demonstrate Yahweh's superiority over the Philistines and their god. The author anticipates the possible objection that all these disasters were simply fortuitous occurrences by having the Philistines themselves raise this possibility and then squelching it with the portentous character of the ark's return. In other words, 1 Sam 6:5–9 is not a later expansion of the ark narrative but an original and very important part of this theological composition.

6:10–16[14]

The story of Yahweh's judgment of Israel and ultimate triumph over Israel's enemy comes to its conclusion in these verses. The point is made clearly *wyšrnh* and emphatically *bmslh 'ḥt* in verse 12 that the cows went directly and immediately to Beth-shemesh. Philistia, in the person of its five lords, witnesses this action (6:16) and knows now that what it has suffered has indeed been at the hand of Yahweh. The narrative, therefore, in its conclusion, continues to direct its attention to the power of the God of Israel rather than to the wanderings of the ark. The ark is at the center of the narrative, but only so that the larger purpose of the story can point to the might and vindication of Yahweh. The ark does not move except as a demonstration of that power. Even the return home is depicted as having its purpose (6:9) and result (6:16) in pointing to and demonstrating that all that has happened has been by the powerful hand of Yahweh of Israel. The appropriate sacrifices and response of joy to Yahweh marks the end of Yahweh's encounter with the Philistines and the return of the ark to Israel.[15]

6:17–18

It is quite possible that verses 17–18a are a secondary expansion of the narrative. Several reasons can be given for that judgment, but none of them is conclusive. The use of *thry* is unusual but not unique in the MT. Ashkelon and Gaza appear here for the first time in the MT, but we have already pointed to the textual evidence that admits the possibility

14. In this section, we follow the MT, except to read *'plyhm* for *tḥryhm* at the end of verse 11 and *lqr'tw* with LXX for *lrwt* at the end of verse 13. On the latter construction, see NAB and the discussion in Driver, *Notes on the Hebrew Text*, 57, where parallel constructions are cited. Note our discussion of a similar emendation in verse 19b. Stoebe, Campbell, and Schicklberger follow the MT, the last on the basis of *lectio difficilior* (*Ladeerzählungen*, 119). The decision can hardly be an absolute and final one in any case. Arguments support both readings.

15. Verse 15 is generally regarded as a secondary insertion that is both repetitive and breaks and contradicts the narrative at points. It is probably a Deuteronomistic gloss, inasmuch as it implies that the stone was not used as an altar, but simply as a place for putting the ark, and insists on giving the leading cultic role to the Levites. See the discussion of Schicklberger, *Ladeerzählungen*, 120–21, and the reasons he gives for the insertion; also Willis, *JBL* 90 (1971), 296 n. 37.

that these two cities were also visited by Yahweh and the ark. Further, the text of verse 18 indicates there were many more golden rats than the five mentioned in the MT of 6:4. But, as we have noted above, the LXX and 4QSam^a omit this phrase in 6:4 and speak only of "golden rats," without specifying the number in 6:5.

With regard to the number of rodents, Wellhausen pointed to the impossibility of forcing such an enormous number of model rats into the box as evidence that this verse is a later expansion of the text, but quite apart from the validity of his calculations, which has been questioned, one must doubt the appropriateness of deciding textual issues on the basis of historical considerations. The ancient author may have given his figures without considering whether all that gold would fit in the vehicle available. Such exaggeration is not the least bit uncommon in Israelite historical narrative.

Finally, one has to raise the obvious question: If the insertion is secondary because of the discrepancies between it and the rest of the narrative, why was an addition to the narrative included when it did not fit on several grounds? We do not propose to resolve the question, but we raise it as a caution in the face of overly hasty suggestions that these verses or parts of them are later glosses on the original narrative.[16]

In their present place in the narrative, the function of verses 17–18a is clear. They are a summary, or more particularly, as Campbell has observed, a list (see *'lh tḥry* [read *'ply*] *hzhb*) of the golden articles to make it clear that they represented all of Philistia, both its lords and all its towns, from fortified cities to unwalled villages and hamlets.

There are some textual problems in verse 18b. The word *'bl* does not make sense in the context. One would expect *h'bn*.[17] In addition, the form *w^e'ad* should probably be repointed to read *w^e'ōd*, as most commentators have suggested. The verse would read, therefore: "The great stone on which the ark of Yahweh was placed is still to this day in the field of Joshua, the Bethshemite." The verse is an etiological note that fits with the concluding and summary character of these verses.

16. For another point of view centering in the interpretation of LXX as a correction to relieve the discrepancies in MT, see Driver, *Notes on the Hebrew Text*, 60–61.

17. So LXX. See the discussions of Driver, Schicklberger, and others.

6:19–7:1

Verse 19b is well nigh hopelessly corrupt in the MT, and it is probably not possible to restore the text with any certainty.[18] Most commentators have regarded the LXX as closer to the original text at several points. The most plausible reconstruction of the text in our judgment—and the one we shall operate with—is that proposed in the textual notes to the Confraternity of Christian Doctrine (NAB) translation and translated in the text: *wᵉlōʾ yiśmᵉḥû* [?] *bᵉnê yekonyāhû* (*bᵉʾanšê bêt šemeš*) *kî qārᵉʾû*, [?] *ʾet ʾᵃrōn* (*yhwh wayyak*) *bāhem* (*šibʿîm ʾîš*),[19] "The descendants of Jeconiah did not join in the celebration with the inhabitants of Beth-shemesh when they greeted the ark of the Lord, and seventy of them were struck down." The reconstruction of *yiśmᵉḥû* for *ēsmenisan* is quite uncertain. This is the only time the word appears in the LXX. An alternative, *ḥādû* has been proposed by some. The reconstruction of *qārᵉʾû* for *rāʾû* is also questionable. The MT is equally plausible at this point.

This final episode is a further demonstration of the power of the God who is enthroned upon the ark. The text that is reconstructed by Cross and Skehan on text-critical grounds fits well in the movement of the narrative and indeed better than some of the translations that seek—with difficulty—to read the MT as it stands. The slaughter of the seventy by Yahweh is not because of a taboo character of the ark that destroys the one who looks inside it.[20] Rather, the destruction is because the sons of Jeconiah did not celebrate the return of the victorious warrior enthroned upon the ark. The words of the men of Beth-shemesh form a kind of theological conclusion to the whole narrative: "Who is able to stand before Yahweh, this holy God?" The answer that is clear from beginning to end is: no one can. At the same time, one may observe that both questions asked in 6:20 get a kind of answer in 6:21 and 7:1. The ark shall go to the house of Abinadab at Kiryath-yearim and Eleazar shall stand before Yahweh to keep the ark. He is sanctified to keep the ark. The verb *šmr* probably has the

18. For discussions of the problems and corruptions in the MT, see Driver, *Notes on the Hebrew Text*, 58–59; Schicklberger, *Ladeerzählungen*, 123ff.

19. Omit *ḥmšym ʾlp ʾyš* with Josephus. It is clearly a gloss.

20. If that is so, then one cannot easily build a case for the original relationship of these verses to 2 Sam 6 on the basis of a common view of the ark, i.e., its taboo power when one touches it or looks into it. The view of the ark and the relationship of Yahweh to it in these closing verses is consistent with the preceding narrative, not 2 Sam 6.

same priestly significance here that it does in those passages that discuss the discharge of priestly functions (Num 1:53; 3:10, etc.).

The story has come full circle. This final episode, in a sense, repeats the plague experience of the Philistines among Israelites.[21] Upon the return of the ark at the end of the narrative, the ark and the power of Yahweh may not be taken for granted any more than it could be at the beginning, in the battle of Ebenezer.

---

21. The following quotation from Willis, *JBL* 90 (1971), 296, is an appropriate conclusion to the exegesis of these chapters, as he indicates the symmetry and interconnectedness of these three chapters with examples that may be added to the numerous ones we have pointed out: "The question of the terror-stricken people of Beth-shemesh ('Who is able to stand before the Lord, this holy God?' 6:20) is strikingly similar to that of the fearful Philistines when they learned that the ark had come into the camp of Israel ('Who can deliver us from the power of these mighty gods?' 4:8). As the Philistines (see above), so also the Beth-shemeshites are 'smitten' (6:19, where the root occurs three times) when the ark comes into their midst. The statement in 6:1, 'the ark of the Lord was in the country of the Philistines seven months,' apparently is intended to be a brief summary of ch. 5 in preparation for ch. 6. The quandary of what to do with the dangerous ark is shared by the Philistines (5:8, 6:2) and the men of Beth-shemesh (6:20). Before they send the ark away, both the Philistines and the Israelites discuss what should be done (5:8, 11; 6:2, 20). As in ch. 5, so also in ch. 6 the Philistines repeatedly express their concern that 'the hand of the Lord be turned away from them' (vss. 3, 5, 9). The golden tumors and the golden mice (6:4, 5, 11, 1718) are 'guilt offerings' corresponding to the plagues of 'tumors' (5:6, 9, 12) and 'mice' (LXX of 5:6; 6:1) which had smitten the Philistines. In view of all this, the coherent theme, the natural sequence of the narrative, and the recurring expressions and terms used in 1 Sam 4:1b–7:1 justify the contention that these chapters (of course, with the occasional exception of a later redactional line or verse, as 6:15) exhibit a symmetry."

7
THE STRUCTURE AND INTENTION OF 1 SAMUEL 2:12–17, 22–25, 27–36; 4:1B–7:1

Having looked at this familiar passage in some detail, one now needs to step back and see in the light of the exegesis and the examination of the extrabiblical backgrounds of the passage what its fundamental character is, for what purpose this artful and highly theological narrative out of Israel's history was crafted. The discussion of the previous chapters, therefore, comes to focus here, as we ask what the story is about and, in the light of our understanding, attempt to place it in the proper context of Israel's faith and history.

It has been our contention from the start that, despite the very fine work of previous scholars (most notably Schicklberger and Campbell), some rather fundamental misapprehensions about the narrative have persisted on a broad—but not unanimous—basis. Fundamental among these is the characterization of these chapters as "the Ark Narrative," with a consequent understanding that is shared by most that the subject matter, the center of attention, and indeed the purpose of the unit is the ark. But to define these chapters as the Ark Narrative(s), qua Rost, Schicklberger, Campbell, and most scholars, is to detheologize them and to miss their point at a most elemental level. The subject of the narrative is *Yahweh*, not the ark. The issue is not what happens to the ark, but what Yahweh is doing among his people. Not the ark, but Yahweh's power and purpose is what the story is about. It is a thoroughly theological narrative at its very core. Indeed, we will argue that it is one of the oldest and most profound theological narratives of the Old Testament.

In the following sections there is some recapitulation of the exegetical conclusions, but only in order to note those thematic and structural elements that hold the passage together and express its intention.

The Structure of the Narrative

I. The Sin of the House of Eli 2:12–17, 22–25, 27–36
   A. The sin proper 12–17
   B. Eli's reprimand 22–25
   C. The announcement of punishment 27–36
      1. Accusation 27–29
      2. Announcement of judgment 30–34
      3. Promise of a faithful priest 35–36

II. The Destruction of the House of Eli 4:1b–22
   A. The battle of Ebenezer 1b–11
      1. Israel brings out the ark 1b–4 (Hophni and Phinehas accompanying)
      2. The Israelites defeated and the ark captured 5–11 (Culminates in the death of Hophni and Phinehas)
   B. The report of the battle 12–22
      1. The report to Eli 12–18 (Culminates in the death of Eli)
      2. The report to Phinehas's wife 19–22 (Culminates in the death of Phinehas's wife)

III. Yahweh's Triumph and the Return of the Ark 5:1–7:1
   A. Yahweh's triumph 5:1–12
      1. Yahweh's war against Dagon 1–5
      2. Yahweh's war against the Philistines 6–12 (The hand of Yahweh)
   B. The return of the ark 6:1–7:1
      1. The Philistine plan to avert the hand of Yahweh 6:1–9
      2. The return of the ark to Beth-shemesh 6:10–16
      3. Summary 6:17–18
      4. Theological and historical conclusion 6:19–7:1

Interpretive Comments on the Structure

I. The Sin of the House of Eli 2:12–17, 22–25, 27–36

The narrative is composed of three major parts, each of which breaks up into definite episodes or stages in the drama that unfolds in this story. The first of these is made up of the verses in chapter 2 that have to do with Eli and his two sons, Hophni and Phinehas. It deals entirely with the sin of the Elides; it both describes the sin and announces the consequent punishment. This part of the narrative provides the motivation for all that follows. It gives an explanation for what would otherwise be an utterly inexplicable event—the defeat of Israel and the seeming defeat of Yahweh at Ebenezer. It not only explains why Israel was defeated but also clarifies the large role that Eli, Hophni, and Phinehas either play in that event or in the reporting of it in this narrative. In doing all of this, these verses also forecast or anticipate matters or elements in the chapters that follow, such as Eli's old age, the death of Hophni and Phinehas on the same day, and the effect that the news of their death has on their father.

The material in this part of the narrative is, therefore, an absolute necessity for understanding the rest of the story, and either these verses or something much like them must be presupposed to set up the narrative that follows.

A. The Sin Proper (2:12–17)

One notes immediately that verses 12 and 17 frame the section, each saying essentially the same thing, one functioning as an introduction to these verses, the other as a conclusion. The focus here is on the description of the sin, the motivating factor for subsequent events in the narrative. That sin revolves around the corruption of the priestly office. The sin is spelled out in detail in terms of practices associated with sacrifice. The passage comes to its climax in verse 17, which clearly is a concluding sentence that summarizes by indicating the extent or greatness of the sin and then in a *kî* causal clause giving a reason why the sin was so terrible, a thoroughly theological reason indicating that the sin was committed directly against God: they treated the offering of the Lord with contempt.

B. Eli's Reprimand (2:22–25)

This unit begins with a reference to Eli's old age, a point that will play an important part in the later events (4:15ff.). Eli indicates the extent of his sons' sin by emphasizing how widely their actions are being voiced abroad. Then he warns them that they are in danger before Yahweh. Verse 25 provides a conclusion to this section that is much like the concluding verse 17 above—a statement of the sons' rejection of the father's warning followed by a *kî* clause giving a theological reason for their attitude: Yahweh had decided to kill them for their sin.

C. The Announcement of Punishment (2:27–36)

The first part (2:12–17, 22–25, 27–36) of this narrative reaches the climax toward which it has been building in these verses. First there was the statement of the sin in actuality and then of the sin theologically interpreted. Then came a warning by the father of the dire consequences of such priestly behavior and a foretelling of what is in Yahweh's mind. Finally comes the explicit and detailed announcement of the punishment that will fall upon the house of Eli, a longer section that appears to have undergone some Deuteronomistic editing but is not originally the work of the Deuteronomistic Historian.

It is couched as a prophetic oracle from an unnamed man of God, a judgment speech with an indictment spelling out the crimes of Hophni and Phinehas and followed by an announcement of judgment that tells of Eli's death and the death of the two sons, as well as of a wider fate for the Elide house. The sign confirming this prophecy to Eli will be the death of Hophni and Phinehas on the same day. The working out of this word in the narrative happens later, in 4:17–18.

The announcement concludes with a divine promise to raise up a faithful priest to replace the faithless ones.

II. The Destruction of the House of Eli 4:1B–22

The problem that has been set up in the first part of the narrative and needs to be dealt with receives its resolution in the second stage of the narrative. How will the punishment announced in chapter 2 happen? Chapter 4 tells us. How will Yahweh's intention to slay Hophni and Phinehas be carried out? Chapter 4 tells us. And what about Eli and the sign to him? All these things are worked out in chapter 4, which tells of the fulfillment of the prophecy of judgment given in chapter 2: Eli and his sons are destroyed. The familiar pattern of prophecy and fulfillment is carried out. That the purpose of this part of the whole narrative is to report that fulfillment and show how Eli, Hophni, and Phinehas died is apparent from the structure.

A. The Battle of Ebenezer (4:1b–11)

This first episode has two movements to it. The initial one (4:1b–4) makes it clear that the issue of *divine power* is fundamental to this whole story. Where is it lodged? What is its meaning? How is it manifest in the affairs of people and nations? These verses give a theological interpretation to the initial defeat—one that is crucial for the whole narrative. They understand their defeat as an act of Yahweh. At the same time, they see it as a testimony to the power (*kap*) of their enemies. The Israelites then seek a theological way out of their dilemma that will overcome the contradiction between the two interpretations of the event, namely, that Yahweh put them to rout and that they were overcome by the power of their enemies. That resolution involves a resort to the ark, whose presence among them will mean Yahweh's presence and his power to save. His power will be greater than that of the Philistines.

Crucial to the movement of the passage and the innerconnectedness of the events is the concluding note that Hophni and Phinehas were with the ark. This datum would be utterly without significance were it not for the prior events of chapter 2. But in the light of what happens and what is said there, its meaning is crystal clear. The presence of these two is an ominous one, for Yahweh has sealed their doom. The next movement in the story will demonstrate that, but here already one sees the potential threat to the ark as well, if Hophni and Phinehas are its caretakers in battle.

The story moves on then to recount what happened when the ark came into the camp. Verses 5–11 are a key passage, signaling and developing various thematic and structural elements. To begin with, the ark is recognized as the manifestation of the presence and power of Yahweh. It will continue to play that role, especially in the denouement in chapters 5 and 6. The question of the Philistines, "Who can deliver us from the power (or hand) of these mighty gods?" is the essential question, one that carries the rest of the narrative and develops the theological intent of the story. It gets an initial, surprising answer in these verses, but one that turns out to be devastatingly short-lived and inaccurate. The question also signals the thematic device that will be the vehicle by which the question of divine power and the intention of the narrative is developed: *the hand of Yahweh.* That is what the Philistines fear, and while the immediate episode seems to indicate its impotence, before the story is finished the hand of Yahweh will smite the Philistines over and over.

Holy-war motifs associated with the coming of the divine warrior to battle with and for Israel are present and contribute to the sense that the passage has to do, not just with the exploits of the ark or an Israelite defeat, but with the divine battle. Continuing that motif is the reference to Yahweh's smiting Egypt with plague and pestilence. It is in just such fashion that Yahweh will smite the Philistines in the next part of this narrative.

In various ways, therefore, the unity of the story and the movement or development of its plot are laid out in verses 5–11. Not least of these is the concluding verse 11, which tells us two facts. One of these—the capture of the ark—points forward, as chapters 5 and 6 deal with the implication and impact of the ark throne of Yahweh in Philistine territory. The second fact is the death of Hophni and Phinehas, which fulfills the prophecy of chapter 2. Both movements (4:1b–4, 5–11) of this first episode, therefore, culminate in words about Hophni and Phinehas, and the episode as a whole culminates in the event toward which the story up to this point has been moving—the death of Eli's sons. These regular concluding references to the sons can hardly be accidental or a matter of indifference to the story. Structurally they are placed at critical junctures, and their significance can hardly be missed by anyone familiar with the first part of the story. Apart from that background, these carefully placed concluding comments carry little, if any, weight or importance. Seen in the light of chapter 2, they are the point of the narrative to this stage.

B. The Report of the Battle (4:12–22)

This second episode, which is also composed of two movements, is transitional. It looks back to what has happened up to this point and deals, therefore, with the fate of the Elides. It also looks forward to the events that take place centering around the ark. In terms of the plot development of the story, what happens is that the initial problem—the sin of the Elides—is resolved. But the resolution of one problem has created another problem of even greater magnitude that tends now to blot out or obscure the former problem. The punishment of the Elides has resulted in the defeat of Israel and the capture of the ark. That now raises into question whether what has been happening is indeed the work of Yahweh or of some other deity. This section already begins to sense that problem (see chart A on page 87).

The place of the episode is, therefore, fairly clear in the overall structure. Both movements are reports to members of the family of Hophni and Phinehas, and both culminate in the death of these members, Eli, and Phinehas's wife. The second movement—the death of Phinehas's wife—makes little sense or has little function in the narrative unless Hophni and Phinehas are central figures, which indeed they are.

As we have already noted, the ark moves more into the forefront in that it is the news of its capture that seems to do in Eli and is the basis of the lament of Phinehas's wife. Here is where the tension in the narrative builds. The deaths of Hophni and Phinehas were to be expected. Eli knew and anticipated the fate of his sons. But the loss of the ark was unexpected and terrifying news. What would otherwise have seemed an understandable outcome of the sins of the Elides turned out to have consequences of much greater and more devastating impact. This further news is so devastating that Eli falls over and breaks his neck—thereby continuing the resolution of the first part of the narrative—and Phinehas's wife laments that the glory—that is, the ark—has departed from Israel.

So the punishment of the Elides has been accomplished, but by the evidence, it looks as if it has not happened through Yahweh's power but as a part of Yahweh's defeat! The story goes on, therefore, to work out the new and apparently greater problem: Was this event the defeat and departure of Yahweh or not? The verses immediately following in chapter 5 will answer that question.

III. Yahweh's Triumph and the Return of the Ark 5:1–7:1

The whole narrative has its climax and denouement in chapters 5 and 6. Here is where it becomes clear once and for all who is in control of this history. This last part of the narrative moves from the Philistine celebration and assertion of victory over Israel and her god to the defeat of the Philistine god and of all the Philistine cities. The ark is at the center of the story, but not merely as the cultic symbol of the Israelites' god. It is at the center as a representation of the presence of Yahweh, a motif just as thoroughly communicating the power of Yahweh as is the hand of Yahweh.

A. Yahweh's Triumph (5:1–12)

The turning point of the narrative is in the first five verses of chapter 5, which describe Yahweh's defeat of the Philistine god. A new stage in the story begins in the first verse. The Philistines celebrate and symbolize their victory by placing the ark, which represents Yahweh, in the temple of Dagon before his statue. The act is meant to be a testimony to the superiority of the Philistine god over the Israelite god. But the Philistines have misread what is happening, and by the time this episode is over, their victory has turned into devastating defeat, first of their god and secondly of the people. By the end of the episode, the Philistines, who had brought the ark proudly into the Dagon sanctuary at the beginning of the episode, want to remove it, not only from the shrine but from the whole territory of Philistia. It has become, not a symbol of Dagon's power over Yahweh and Israel, but of Yahweh's power over Dagon and the Philistines (see chart B on page 88).

While the visible symbol of Yahweh's power and presence here is the ark, the invisible manifestation of that same power and presence is *the hand of Yahweh*. The ark and the hand of God are the principal thematic elements and vehicles for the divine agency. We have elaborated at length upon the role of the hand of Yahweh in the story, and there is no need to repeat that in detail here. It was the hand of "these mighty gods" that the Philistines had feared at Ebenezer. The hand of Dagon seemed to have been more powerful until it was cut off by Yahweh, whose hand then cut a path of destruction through the Philistine cities (see chart B). In chapter 4 as well as in chapters 5 and 6, the hand of Yahweh is associated both with the exodus events and with the experience of plagues and pestilence. It is a symbol of the divine warrior Yahweh who battles with his enemies, human and divine, and defeats them.

B. The Return of the Ark (6:1–7:1)

A transition or dividing point is made with the chronological note in verse 1. In this new episode, the narrative shifts to tell about the Philistine plan to remove the ark of the God of Israel and thus avert his destructive power. The hand of Yahweh is again the thematic note sounded throughout the first part of the episode. As in the preceding section, the hand of Yahweh is referred to three times (6:3, 5, and 9). The whole intention of the consultation with the priests and diviners is to remove the hand of Yahweh (see discussion of 6:3). In verse 5, the theological rationale for the guilt-offering images is stated in terms of the hand of the God of Israel. Such action may remove the hand both from the people (referring back to 5:6–12) and their gods (referring back to 5:1–5). As verse 9 indicates, the narrative in this section seeks to make unmistakably clear that all that has happened is due not to chance but to the hand of Yahweh. If that is not evident, then the narrative would not accomplish its fundamental purpose of affirming the superiority of Yahweh over the enemies of Israel and their gods. The device to confirm Yahweh's agency in all these events is provided by the Philistines themselves. It is planned and devised in verses 1–9. It is carried out in verses 10–16 and, indeed, confirms to all Philistia (6:16: the five lords) that their fate has not been fortuitous but has been determined by Yahweh's action and purpose.

The place of the summary (6:17–18) in the overall structure and movement of the passage is clear. Whether or not it is a secondary expansion, this list serves to underscore the point that what has happened has been the fate of all Philistia and thus, by implication, that Yahweh's defeat of the Philistines has been total.

The narrative concludes with what seems at first glance to be an episode unrelated to the overall movement of this story and one that has often been regarded as manifesting a different view of the ark. In our exegetical comments we have tried to show why neither initial assumption is correct. The return of the ark is not simply the return of a receptacle, nor is this section merely a historical footnote to the ark wanderings that serves to explain how it got from Beth-shemesh to Kiryath-yearim. It does do the latter, but only as a part of the overall intention. The return of the ark is the return of the divine warrior who has demonstrated his might and vindicated his power over his and Israel's enemies. The response can only be celebration, and those who do not respond in this way also feel the hand of the divine warrior. The men of Beth-shemesh, like the Philistines, give a final testimony to the power of Yahweh (6:20); this has been the point of the whole narrative: no one can stand before the power of this God (see 4:8)—a lesson learned well by Dagon and the inhabitants of the Philistine pentapolis but applicable to the Israelites also. There is another answer, however, to the initial question of the men of Beth-shemesh. So in a double question and answer the narrative comes to its close.

Question	**Answer**
1. Who can stand before Yahweh?	Implicit—no one Explicit—Eleazar
2. Where shall we send the ark?	Kiryath-yearim

CHART A

Problem		**Resolution**			
sin of the Elides	→	death of the Elides			
		↓	**New Problem**		**Resolution**
			defeat of Israel; loss of the ark	→	defeat of Dagon and Philistines; return of the ark

CHART B

Expected	**Surprise**
Yahweh's hand victorious (4:1b–9)	Philistines (i.e., Dagon's hand) victorious (4:10–11)
Expected	**Surprise**
Yahweh defeated; Dagon's hand victorious (5:1–2)	Dagon's hand cut off and Yahweh victorious (5:3–5 and rest of story)

The Theological Intention of the Narrative

We have argued that, from beginning to end, these chapters in 1 Samuel are a thoroughgoing theological narrative. At their center are the motifs of the divine battle and the capture and return of divine images; one motif belongs to the mythology of the ancient Near East, the other to the historical practices of warfare (and carries very important religious connotations). We have examined both of these aspects of the story—as well as others—in the light of comparative mythologies and practices to illumine their particular intention in the story as a whole and their contribution to the purpose of the narrative as a whole. The structural analysis has also confirmed the intention of the narrative and its theological character.

The impetus for the events and the story is the sin of Israel's leaders, the Elides, the priests of Israel. Their contempt for the holiness of Yahweh and the responsibilities of serving him in the sacrificial cultus calls down his judgment in an event that engulfs the whole people: the defeat of the Israelites at the battle of Ebenezer. Despite the suggestion often made in the literature—but no less superficial for its frequent repetition—that chapters 4–6 have no connection with chapters 1–3, the events of the later chapters can only be understood as growing out of the significant sin of the priests described in chapter 2. In every part of chapter 4 the narrator makes the point that Hophni and Phinehas are the key figures involved. Each section or episode of that chapter culminates in a reference to one of the Elides. The ark is lost because those accompanying it are the faithless sons of Eli. In the unexpected (according to the narrative) and overwhelming defeat by the Philistines, the narrator concludes by reporting the death of Hophni and Phinehas. The remaining sections have as their focus the deaths of the father and the wife of Phinehas upon hearing the reports of the death of the wicked priests and the loss of the ark.

All of this makes clear and inescapable that the narrator is showing how the divine intention to punish and slay the Elides (2:25 and 30ff.) was wrought out in this event. No literary-critical moves or redactional analysis can fully eliminate this dimension of chapter 4 without simply destroying the integrity and intelligibility of the narrative. Chapters 2:12ff. and 4 are a familiar account of human sin and divine punishment, the latter (as is often the case) happening in the subsequent historical events surrounding the ones under judgment. One may compare in this respect the so-called Throne Succession document in 2 Samuel and 1 Kings, where once again Rost may have misled us by attaching to it a title that belies its highly theological character, indeed an intention much like that of the narrative under consideration here. In 2 Sam 12:7ff., a prophet announces to David the judgment of God against him for his sin in the Bathsheba incident (cf. 1 Sam 2:27ff.). The rest of that story shows the working out of that word of judgment without direct reference back to the original announcement of judgment.

But in the course of the working out of the problem of the sinful leaders of Israel, a new problem arose or seemed to arise, the resolution of which becomes the focus of the rest of the narrative. The great defeat at Ebenezer called in question in radical fashion the power and claims of Yahweh of Israel. The battle itself would have done that, but inasmuch as one of the major results of the defeat was the loss of the ark (the throne and dwelling place of Yahweh), the significance of the event for the question of who was in control of history became all the sharper. Israel would have seen the events of that time, not as a demonstration of the working out of the word of Yahweh in history, but as a sign of his powerlessness in the historical arena. The narrator sets up the story to reflect this perspective in 4:5–9 with a question—"Who can deliver us from the hand of these mighty gods?"—and a recall of the power of the Israelite god(s) against the Egyptians. The question and accompanying historical reference are a clear lament implying an answer: no one can deliver us. But the events that follow imply that someone mightier, another stronger hand, did indeed deliver them. One can only infer that the mightier one was the Philistine (Canaanite) deity, Dagon.

It is because of the apparent—but nevertheless erroneous—conformity of the above analysis to the actual events that the turning point of the narrative is found in 1 Sam 5:1–5, and the rest of the narrative (after the death of the Elides) centers around the meaning of the capture and return of the divine "representation," the ark. As we have indicated, various possibilities were available for the interpretation of the capture of the ark. The most prominent and most likely among them (besides the view that Yahweh had been defeated and made subject to the Philistine god[s]) was the view that Yahweh had abandoned his people in anger (cf. the later visions of Ezekiel). But the narrative at no point proposes such an interpretation of this seemingly catastrophic event. Indeed, the defeat was not due to Yahweh's anger at *Israel* but was the means by which his judgment of the religious leaders was accomplished. Until chapter 5, however, and indeed, reinforced by the opening verses of that chapter, one is led to believe that Philistine might and the might of their god have brought about the defeat of Israel and her god.

Between verses 1 and 4 of 1 Sam 5, this story moves from its low point to its climax, and we find the first conflict of the gods in the history of Israel's religion—or at least, that which is implicit elsewhere now becomes largely explicit. This brief section begins with Yahweh's ark being brought in to stand alongside Dagon as a captured god and an object of worship with Dagon.

In two verses—matter-of-factly, obliquely, yet without doubt—it then recounts the results of Yahweh's victory over and slaughter of Dagon, culminating in the cutting off of his head and hands. The hand of Dagon is thus rendered powerless before the hand of Yahweh. The expected but seemingly erroneous answer to the lament of 4:8 (no one can deliver us) is now seen to be indeed the correct one. The apparent victor is now the defeated one.

The encounter between Yahweh and the gods of Canaan has its first round in this episode.[1] It is thus a precursor of the conflict that becomes full-blown and manifests itself widely in the history of the two kingdoms, although the point of the encounter here is not the struggle for the allegiance of Israel, as it is later, but the manifestation of Yahweh's power over Israel's historical enemies in the earlier period. These verses present us with the ancient mythological motif of the battle of the gods and the victory of the divine warrior Yahweh. Only in this case, the motif appears in a prosaized, nonmythological context. We do not have here a poetic

1. That is not to say that there may not have been manifestations of that encounter earlier, but in the existing narrative account of the early history of Israel, this is where one comes upon it.

recounting of divine victory as in the early poetry, but rather a carefully structured prose narrative, the heart of which is in this episode in 1 Sam 5 and the events that grow out of it. The prose narrative character of the story presumably contributes to the way in which the divine battle is reported, that is, the Philistine discovery of what happened to the statue of Dagon. In this period one would expect a recounting of the actual battle in mythopoeic, poetic form rather than prose. But the battle lies behind and is to be presupposed in this prose narrative. The incident of these five verses is rooted in Canaanite mythology—more so than usually acknowledged—but at the same time, in typically Israelite fashion, it is "demythologized," both by the way in which the report of battle comes to us and by the fact that the intent of the mythological cosmic battle is lost. Here it is not life against death, fertility against sterility, order against chaos, the young god against the old god. It is Yahweh against the gods of Israel's enemies and ultimately it is Yahweh overcoming the enemies themselves.

The rest of the narrative can be said to be simply a working out of the implications of Yahweh's victory in the temple at Ashdod. The divine warrior marches in battle through the Philistine pentapolis wreaking havoc by plague and pestilence against the enemies of Israel until they are thoroughly defeated and Yahweh's rule over the history of those times is thoroughly and convincingly demonstrated. His power is vindicated, and the story becomes a caution against misreading history or the hand of Yahweh in it. Seeming defeat is now seen to be the mysterious working out of God's power over history. From beginning to end all that has happened has been the hand of Yahweh at work. The judgment of the faithless leaders is accomplished. The enemies of his people are defeated.

The only way in which it is legitimate to view these chapters as an ark narrative in intention as well as subject matter is to recognize that in this narrative we have an early theodicy, that is, the vindication of the ways of Yahweh. How does one account for the great defeat of the people of Yahweh and the loss of their central cultic symbol, the throne of the deity? The answer is given in the story. It was not the defeat of Yahweh, as it may have seemed. Rather, the whole thing was Yahweh's purpose. As always in the resolution of theodicy, one must have insight into that larger purpose to understand the present disaster.

One final question remains with regard to this narrative that relates directly to its intention: When was it composed? Some who have maintained, as we have, that 2 Sam 6 is not an integral part of the narrative, have argued that the narrative in 1 Sam 4–6 grew out of the more historical and earlier account in 2 Sam 6.[2] In our judgment, such an interpretation does not satisfactorily explain the present character of the story as we have analyzed it. After David's decisive defeat of the Philistines and the restoration of the ark, there would be little point in formulating the ark material as has been done in 1 Sam 2:12ff.; 4–6. The theological problem of Israel's defeat at Ebenezer would no longer have been a real problem. By analogy with the Mesopotamian parallels, one could have dealt with it quite simply. Yahweh became angry with his people and in his anger deserted them for a time. But finally, when his anger had passed and a pious king had come to the throne of Israel, he commissioned that king to carry out his punishment on the wicked Philistines and to return his ark to its proper place. If Yahweh could commission Saul to execute his vengeance on the Amalekites, there is no reason why he could not have used David in executing his vengeance on the Philistines after the defeat at Ebenezer—particularly if it were David's victories over the Philistines that restored Kiryath-yearim to full Israelite control and permitted David to move the ark to Jerusalem. Against the background of the Near Eastern parallels, it is certainly striking that 1 Sam 4–6 gives David no part in Yahweh's victory over the Philistines, especially when one compares the tradition in 2 Sam 5:17–21, which *does* give David a major role in Yahweh's defeat of the Philistines and their idols.

We have sought to show that this narrative deals with the fundamental problem of who is supreme, who is God: Yahweh or Dagon. In this respect, it is parallel to the contest between Elijah and the prophets of Baal on Mount Carmel. In the case of the story before us, however, the theological problem has been posed by a historical event, the Israelite defeat at Ebenezer and the shocking loss of the ark. Prior to David's imperial expansion, one could see how this would pose a serious problem to Israel's faith. If the ark were still sitting in the temple of Dagon or even if it had been returned to a border area where it was still under some Philistine control, one could see how an Israelite might be tempted to regard Dagon as Yahweh's superior. In that setting one can understand the need for a

---

2. K. D. Schunck, *Benjamin* (BZAW 86; Berlin: Töpelmann, 1963), 97–101. Cf. Th. C. Vriezen, "Die Compositie van de Samüel-Boeken," *Orientalia Neerlandica* (Leiden: Sijthoff, 1948), 167–86; and the discussion in Campbell, *Ark Narrative*, 42ff.

theological counterattack. This superficial interpretation of the revelation in history would have to be replaced by another that demonstrated Yahweh's superiority. After David's imperial expansion and subjugation of the Philistines, however, this serious theological problem would not exist. Once the tables were turned and the Philistines had to send tribute up to Jerusalem to David and his god, Yahweh, why would any Israelite think Dagon was superior? History would already have vindicated Yahweh's superiority! And if the problem were discussed, one would expect it to have been resolved by the citation of the actual course of events, as we in fact have it in 2 Sam 5:21.

In other words, the formulation of this narrative belongs to the period of religious crisis between the disastrous defeat at Ebenezer and the much later victories of David. Israel was probably too stunned at first to offer any explanation, and extrapolating from the much later material around the fall of Jerusalem, one can imagine that the faith of many was shaken to its foundations. Some months later, when the ark was returned to Israelite territory, this unexpected turn of events provided the starting point for a whole new way of looking at the shattering events that had befallen Israel. Even if the ark were still under nominal Philistine control, the Israelite theologian could see its return as a sign of Yahweh's victory over the Philistines, particularly if this return coincided with a serious plague in Philistine territory. There would, of course, be doubters, those who could see no connection between the Philistine's return of the ark and any victory of Yahweh. It would be precisely such objections that forced the theologian to underline the cause-and-effect relationship between the ark and the plague, insisting that it was no accident that the Philistines started dying just when they did. There would be a tendency to exaggerate the magnitude of the plague, and because the theological question of who was God was tied up with the fate of a concrete cultic symbol, there would be pressure to erase the infamy of the ark's capture by a corresponding, but worse, degradation of Dagon's symbol, a degradation that clearly indicated Dagon's defeat. In this way the legend of Dagon's collapse before the ark was formulated, and to buttress this story the theologian added the etiology in verse 5: "If you do not believe this, go see for yourself. The priests of Dagon still skip over the threshold."

The whole narrative was not created immediately after the return of the ark. One must assume that the legend grew and developed in response both to doubt and to the storyteller's art, and it was probably affected as well by the growing distance from the historical events. Some elements, such as the etiology, could even be a much later addition, but, in essence, the narrative was formulated before David's victories removed the theological problem that created the need for it.

APPENDIX

Since some of the cuneiform texts referred to in our discussion have not been translated recently and are edited only in older works not readily available to the average Old Testament scholar, we have included a transliteration and translation of them in this appendix. Only the directly relevant portion of text 1 is treated, and text 6, a composite restoration of a few lines from two apparent duplicates, is offered in transcription and translation. Otherwise the texts are presented in full. The transliterations are given as a control on our translation, but as this treatment is not intended as an edition for Assyriologists, no notes have been added. For further bibliography on each text, consult Rykle Borger, *Handbuch der Keilschriftliteratur* (3 vols.; Berlin: de Gruyter, 1967–1975).

Text 1: V *R* 33 I, 44–II, 17

^{44} i-nu Marduk (^{d}AMAR.UTU) ^{45} bēl(EN) É-sag-íl ^{46} ù Babili(KÁ.DINGIR.RA^{ki}) ^{47} ilū(DINGIR) rabūtu(GAL.GAL.LA) ^{48} i-na pi-i-šu-nu el-lim ^{49} a-na Babili(KÁ.DINGIR.RA^{ki}) ^{50} ta-a-a-ar-šú iq-bu-u ^{51} Marduk (^{d}AMAR.UTU) ana(DIŠ) Babili(DIN.TIR^{ki}) ^{52} [x] x pa-ni-šú iš-ku-na ^{53} [ ] la? Marduk(^{d}AMAR.UTU) ^{54} [ ] x a a ^{II} ^{1}ak-pú-ud at-ta-id-ma ^{2} a-na le-qé-e Marduk(^{d}AMAR.UTU) ^{3} a-na Babili(KÁ.DINGIR.RA^{ki}) ^{4} pa-ni-šu áš-kun-ma ^{5} tap-pu-ut Marduk(^{d}AMAR.UTU) ^{6} ra-im palêya(BAL-e-a) ^{7} al-lik-ma ^{8} šarra(LUGAL) Šamaš(^{d}UTU) ina(AŠ) šamān(Ì.GIŠ) bārî (^{lù}ḪAL) a-šal-ma ^{9} a-na māt(KUR) ruq-ti a-na māt(KUR) Ḫa-ni-i ^{10} lu-ú áš-pur-ma qat(ŠU) Marduk (^{d}AMAR.UTU) ^{11} ù ^{d}Ṣar-pa-ni-tum ^{12} lu iṣ-ba-tu-nim-ma ^{13} Marduk(^{d}AMAR.UTU) ù ^{d}Ṣar-pa-ni-tum ^{14} ra-im palêya (BAL-e-a) ^{15} a-na É-sag-íl ^{16} ù Babili(KÁ.DINGIR.RA^{ki}) ^{17} lu ú-tir-šu-nu-ti

When the great gods by their pure mouth commanded the return of Marduk, lord of Esagil and Babylon, to Babylon, Marduk set his face [to go] to Babylon. [...].. Marduk [...]. Obeying, I made plans and set out to take Marduk to Babylon, thereby assisting Marduk who loves my rule. After consulting king Šamaš by the oil of the diviner, I wrote to a distant land, the land Hana, that they might take the hand of Marduk and Sarpanitum. Thus I returned Marduk and Sarpanitum who loves my rule to Esagil and Babylon.

Text 2: *CT* 13, 48

(1) a-šib i-na Babili (KÁ.DINGIR.RA^{ki}) Nabu-kudurrī uṣur(^{d}AG NÍG.DU-URÙ)
(2) il-tam-mir ki-i nē š u(UR.MAḪ) ki-i Adad (^{d}IM) i-šag-[gu-um]
(3) rabūtīšu(^{lú}GAL.MEŠ-šú) e-du-ú–tu ki-ma la-ab-bu u-šag[-lat]
(4) a-na Marduk(^{d}AMAR.UTU) bēl(EN) Babili(DIN.TIR^{ki}) il-la-ku su-pu-ú-[šú]
(5) a-ḫu-lap at-tu-ú-a šu-ta-nu-ḫu ù ú-tu- [ ]
(6) a-ḫu-lap i-na mātīya(KUR-ya) šaknū(GAR) ba-ke-e ù sa-pa-a-d[u]
(7) a-ḫu-lap i-na nišīya(UN.MEŠ-ya) šaknū(GAR) nu-um-be-e a-ba-ke-e
(8) [a]-di ma-ti bēl(EN) Babili(DIN.TIR^{ki}) ina(AŠ) māti(KUR) na-ki-ri áš-ba-a-ti
(9) [li]b?-bal-[k]it i-na lib-bi-ka Babili(DIN.TIR^{ki}) ba-nu-um-ma
(10) [a-n]a E-sag-íl šá ta-ram-mu šu-us-ḫi-ra pa-ni-ka
(11) [?]x[?] Nabu-kudurrī uṣur(^{d}AG-NÍG.DU-URÙ) bēl(EN) Babili(KÁ.X.DINGIR.RA^{ki}) iš-mé-e-ma
(12) [amat? u]l-tu šamê(AN-e) in-da-naq-qu-ta-áš-ši
(13) (at tu a? i]-na pi-i aq-bak-ka a-na-ku
(14) [x x x x] x šá du-un-qa al-ta-tap-pa-rak-ka
(15) [x x x x x] x-ya te-ba-a-ta a-na māt Amurri(KUR MAR.TU^{ki})
(16) [x x x x x a?]-mat? ṭè-me-ka ši-me
(17) [x x? ul-tu Ela]mti ([NI]M.MA^{ki}) a-na Babili[KÁ.DINGIR.RA^{ki}) li-qa-an-nu
(18) [a-na-ku bēI(EN) Bab]ili(KÁ].DINGIR.RA^{ki} Elamtu(NIM.MA^{ki}) [l]ud-din-ak-ka
(19) [x x x x x] x-ka e-li-ti ù šá-pil-ti
(20) [a-na Elamti(NIM.MA]^{ki}) iṣ-ṣa-bat [Ḫarrān(KASKAL)?] ilānīšu (DINGIR.MEŠ-šú)
(21) . . . . (The rest is broken off.)

(1) [Valiant?] Nebuchadnezzar dwells in Babylon.
(2) He roars like a lion, like Adad he thunders.
(3) His renowned nobles he frightens like a lion.
(4) To Marduk, lord of Babylon, goes his prayer:
(5) "Be merciful! For me there is dejection and ....
(6) Be merciful! In my land there is weeping and mourning.
(7) Be merciful! Among my people there is wailing and weeping.
(8) How long, O lord of Babylon, will you dwell in an enemy land?
(9) Remember Babylon the well-favored. (Literally: Let Babylon the well-favored cross over into your heart.)
(10) To Esagil which you love turn your face."
(11) The lord of Babylon heard the [prayer] of Nebuchadnezzar;
(12) A [message?] from heaven keeps falling down to him:
(13) "With [my own] mouth I myself have spoken to you.
(14) [A message] of favor I have been sending you.
(15) [ ] my[ ] you have gone up against the land of Amurru.
(16) [ ] hear the message (I have) for you:
(17) [?] I from Elam fetch me home to Babylon.
(18) [I, the lord of Baby]lon, will give you Elam.
(19) [Victorious/Majestic/Unrivaled? will be your [...?] everywhere."
(20) [Toward Ela]m he took [the road] of his gods.

Text 3: IV *R* 20, 1; *AJSL*, 35, 139, Ki. 1904–10–9, 96

(1) [x x x x x x x x] e? KU? ní.bi.ta nam.kur.re.e.ne ug$_5$.ga.gin$_x$ šèg.šèg giš.tukul á.bi lál.e LÚ.Ú Š.a.ni sal.la.ke$_4$

(2) [x x x x x x] ma-la ik-šu-du-uš kakki(GIŠ.TUKUL) ina(AŠ) ra-ma-ni-šú-nu ki-ma mi-tu-ut ḫal-pe-e i-di-šú-nu uk-tas-sa-ma mu-uṣ-ṣu-u šal-mat-su-un

(3) [an.ta ki.t]a á.zi.da ágùb.bu igi egir a.má.uru$_5$ mu.un.dib.eš.am uru šà.ba uru bar.ra edin edin.na sìg.sìg bí.in.si a.ri.a mu.un.gin.gin

(4) [e-liš ù šap-liš] im-na ù šu-me-la pa-ni ù ar-ku uš-bi-'a-bu-ba-niš-ma libbi(ŠÀ) āli(URU) a-ḫat āli(URU) ṣ-i-ru ba-ma-a-ti šá-qu-um-ma-tu ú-šam-li-ma ú-šá-li-ka na-mu-iš

(5) [gú.ki.gál? ù.gul?] gá.gá še.še.ga lú.igi.du$_8$.a.bi sag.uš ab.ta.bu.bu.lu en.e šà.ba.a.ni na.me mu.un.BU.i šà.ne.ša$_4$ nam.mi.in.gub

(6) [x] [rle ši pa x iḫ x x x[mut]-nen-nu-u mu-un-dag-ri šá ana(DIŠ) ta-mar-ti-šú kak-da-a pu-tuq-qu-ma a-di ú-šam-ṣu-šú ma-la lib-bu-uš la ik-la-a un-nin-ni

(7) [en.le i.bí bar.ra alam sukud.da.a.ni u$_4$. šú.uš.e múš.nu.túm.ma su.gurum.ma su.mu nu.kud.da úr.ra.a.ni ge$_6$ dùg.ga.bi nu.til.la.e.da.ni ù.sá.na.nam

(8) [a]-di at-tap-la-su la-an-šu e-la-a u$_4$-mi-šam la na-par-ka-a zur-ri qid-da-a-ti ina(AŠ) zu-um-ri-ya la ip-par-su-ú-ma ina(AŠ) ut-lu mu-ši ṭa-a-bu la ú-qat-ta-a šit-ti

(9) [ ] mu.un.gig.ga.mu šud$_x$(KAxŠU).de kúš.ù.mu šu.íl.la.mu u$_4$.šú.uš.e kir$_4$ šu.mar.ra.mu sizkur$_x$.ra.a.ni ù.gul.gá.gá šà.bi damal.la arḫuš tug.a gú.bi nigin šà.bi.ta uru kù.ga

(10) [u]n-nin-ni-ya šum-ru-ṣu-ti ik-ri-bi-ya šu-nu-ḫu-ti ni-iš qa-ti-ya ù la-ban ap-pi-ya šá u$_4$-mi-šam a-bal-lu-uš ut-nin-nu-šú

(11) [ṣu]r-ru-uš šad-lì re-e-mu ir-ši-ma ki-šad-su ú-sa ḫ-ḫi-ra ana (DIŠ) qí-rib āli(URU) elli(KÙ.GA)

(12) [š]a.bi túm.ma a.ra uru.gibil mu.un.gin.a.ni šà.bi.ta níg.ḫul NIM.ma^{ki}.ke$_4$ kaskal a.li.ri ḫar.ra.an asilal ḫé.en.da še.še.ga šà.šu.an.na.ta mu.un.dib

(13) šá ub-la lìb-ba-šú a-lak URU.GIBIL^{ki} i-ku-šam-ma iš-tu qí-rib lem-né-ti e-lam-ti ḫar-ra-anšu-lu-lu! ú-ru-uḫ ri-šá-a-ti

(14) ṭu!-da-at taš-me-e ù ma-ga-ri iṣ-ba-ta ana(DIŠ) qí-rib Babili(ŠU.AN.NA^{ki})

(15) un ma.da igi.kár.kár.ra.ab é.gar$_8$.bi sukud.da ḫé.du$_7$ še.ir.ma.al šu.li.li.eš bar.damal.la da.gan.bi ur$_5$ ra.ag.a.e.ne

(16) ib-tar-ra-a ni-ši ma-a-ti la-an-šú e-la-a šu-su-mu e-til-la na-par-da-a šu-lu-la kul-lat-si-na pu-tuq-qa-šu

(17) nam.ba.ni.íb.sun$_x$.na ù.mu.un ba.ni.in.ri dul.mar.ra bí ní.dúb.dúb.bu

(18) i-ru-um-ma be-lum ir-ta-me šu-bat-su ni-iḫ-ta

(19) ká.su.lim nam.lugal.la.bi.šè é.šà.sìg.ga gìr.gá ba.ni.íb.si.sá.e me.li ár.i.i

(20) bāb šalummati(KÁ.SU.LIM) pa-paḫ be-lu-ti-šú im-me-ra ma-li ri-šá-a-ti

(21) an.ki.bi.ta du$_8$.du$_8$.bi.e.ne a.ab.ba za.ba.lam.a.ni si.ba.ni.íb.sá ḫur.sag máš mu.un.da.ri.bi

(22) šá-mu-ú ḫé-en-gal la-šú-nu er-ṣe-tum ḫi-ṣib-šá tam-tum mi-ḫir-ta-šá šá-du-ú i-rib-šú

(23) sizkur$_x$.bi.ne.ne èm i.bí nu.mu.un.bar.ra níg a.na eme inim bal.bal.e

(24) kit-ru-ba-áš-šú šú-ut la maḫ-ra ma-la šu-un-na-a li-šá-a-nu

(25) mu.un dugud.da.bi mu.un.ši.in.íl.íl.eš ù.mu.un lugal.la.šè ka-bit-ti bi-lat-su-nu na-šu-ú a-na be-el be-lu$_4$

(26) e.lu bí.in.šum.mu.dè.eš gud.gal.gal.la bí.in.šár.šár.ra nig.KU.DU.ul

mu.un.ši.in.gál.le.eš na.izi bí.in.si.si

(27) as-lu ṭu-ub-bu-ḫu du-uš-šu-ú gu$_4$ maḫ-e zi-i-bu šur-ru-ḫu ṣe-e-ni qut-rin-na

(28) ir.si.im mi.ni.in.è ir.sim bi.in.d[u$_{10}$]

(29) ar man nu uš-te-iṣ-˹ṣa-a˺ i-ri-še ṭa-bu-ú

(30) sizkur$_x$ dili.dili[ ] in.du$_8$.du$_8$ me.li gal si ba.ni.íb.si

(31) ni-qí e-[ ] ti na-qí ˹ma˺-li ri-šá-a-ti

(32) [ ] dak.ka.ni nam mu.un.ši.in.gágá

(33) [ ] diš du u ta-šil-ta šak-na-at

(34) [ ]x zú.NE.NE.ra.bi igi.du$_8$ gu$_4$.ud ^{d}asar.ri.ke$_4$

(35) [ilū(DINGIR.MEŠ)? šá-m]a-me u qaq-qa-ri ṣi-ḫi-iš i˹na-a˺ṭ-ṭa-lu Marduk(^{d}AMAR.UTU) qar-du

(1–2) [ ] as many as the weapon touched—their arms became stiff by themselves like those who die of cold, and their corpses were spread about.

(3–4) [Above and below], right and left, forward and backward he caused to sweep through like a flood. The center of the city, the outskirts of the city, the open country and the hill country he filled with ghostly silence; he made them like the steppe.

(5–6) [ ] the prayerful one, the compliant one, who constantly waited for his appearance, did not cease praying until he had satisfied his heart's desire.

(7–8) Until I had seen his exalted form, every day my … was unceasing, bowing down did not depart from my body, and in the sweet embrace of the night I did not finish out my sleep.

(9–11) [Because of] my ardent supplications, my strenuous invocations, my prayers, and my gestures of submission with which I daily besought him in prayer, his generous heart became merciful and he turned back to the pure city.

(12–14) As his heart desired to go to Babylon he came, and from the midst of wicked Elam he took a road of cheering, a way of joy, a path of of homage and acceptance towards Babylon.

(15–16) The people of the land kept staring at his tall, majestic, lordly stature; acclaiming his brilliance, all of them stood at attention for him.

(17–18) The lord entered and settled down in his restful abode.

(19–20) The gate of splendor, the cella of his lordship shone, it was full of joy.
(21–22) The heavens (offer) their yield, the earth its abundance, the sea its tribute, the mountain its produce.
(23–24) As many languages as there are, they invoke him, the one who is unrivaled.
(25) Their heavy tribute they bring to the lord of lords.
(26–27) Fine sheep are slaughtered, grown bulls and food offerings are provided in abundance, incense is heaped up.
(28–29) The *armannu*-wood gives off a sweet fragrance.
(30–33) (Too broken for connected translation.)
(34–35) [The gods … of hea]ven and earth with happy laughter gaze at Marduk, the valiant.

Text 4: DT 71

(1) [ ]
(2) [ ] tap? ri? [ ]
(3) [ ] x UD e
(4) [ ] -de-e-šú
(5) [i-lut-su lud-b]u-ba [da]n-nu-us-su
(6) [q]u-ru-us-su lud-lul
(7) [i-]lut-su lud-bu-ba dan-nu-us-su
(8) [ ] šú qu-ru-us-su lud-lul
(9) [ta-]a-a-ru ša na-as-ḫur-šú qer-bu
(10) [ ]a-a līssu(TE-su) id-da-a iš-ku-na sa-li-mu
(11) [ip-ša-aḫ ?]lìb-ba-šú ir-šú-ú ta-a-a-ru
(12) [iś-mu -]ú un-nin-ni-ya ú-saḫ-ḫi-ra ki-šad-su
(13) [ka-bat-s]u! ip-šá-ḫa ir-ša-a sa-li-mu
(14) [e-la-m]u-ú ša la pit-lu-ḫu rabitu(GAL-tu) ilūssu(DINGIR-us-su
(15) [eli (UGU)] ilūtīšu(DINGIR-ti-šú) ṣir-tu iq-bu-ú me-ri-iḫ-tu
(16) [ ]-us-su kakkīka(GIŠ.TUKUL-ka) a-na e-la-me-e muš-tar-ḫi
(17) [tu-sap-pi-iḫ?] ummanātīšu(ERIM$^{ḫi.a}$-šú) tu-par-ri-ir el-lat-su
(18) [nišīšu(UN.MEŠ-š]ú) di-šá-a-ti tu-bal-li la-’-meš
(19) [-šú r]abâ([G]AL-a) a-bu-ba-niš tas-pu-un
(20) [da-ad-me-šú t]u-šaḫ-ri-ba tu-šá-ad-di māssu(KUR-su)
(21) [ālānīšu(URU.MEŠ-]š[ú)] tas-pu-na til-la-niš tu-tir
Rev.
(1) [ilāni(DINGIR.MEŠ) šá šá-’-lu

(2) [ ]x kar-pa-niš taḫ-pi
(3) [ ]ti šu-uḫ-ru-bat ekurru(É.KUR)
(4) [ ]nin-da-bu-u pa-ri-is-ma
(5) [ ] la-mas-su-uš it-ri
(6) [še-du d]a-me-eq-šú šu-up-pu-uḫ
(7) [ ] šu-ku-lat Girra(^{d}GIŠ.BAR)
(8) [ ]x kar-pa-niš taḫ-pi
(9) [ ]x palâšu(BAL-a-šú) tas-kip
(10) [ ]x ú-šar-ri-ḫa ra-man-šú
(11) [ ]x it-tak-lu e-mu-qu
(12) [l]a iḫ-su-sa ilūtka(DINGIR-ut-ka)
(13) [ik]-šu-du-uš kakkīka(GIŠ.TUKUL-ka)
(14) [ ]x māt(KUR) nu-kúr-ti ú-ab-bit
(15) [ ] el-ṣi-iš tu-par-ri-ir
(16) [tu-ha]l-li-qa ni-ip-ri-šú
(17) [ ]palâšu (BAL-a-šú) tas-kip
(18) [ ] za-ma-na-a tu-hal-liq
(19) [ ] zi-kir-ka kab-tu$_4$
(20) [ ]ḫu la? aṣ-ṣu-ru ma-mit-su
(21) [ ]ḫu tu-bal-li la-’meš
(22) [ ] dan-nu-us-su
(23) [ ] zi-kir-šú
(24) [ ] mug-da-aš-ru
(25) [ ] re-ṣu-ú-ti
(26) [ ] za-’-i-ri-ya
(27) [ ] zi-kir-š[ú]
(28) [ ] pa x [ ]
(29) [ ]

(1–4) Only traces remain.
(5) [I will magnify (?) his divinity, I will sp]eak of his might.
(6) [I will sing of (?) his …], his valor I will praise.
(7) [I will magnify (?)] his divinity, I will speak of his might.
(8) [I will sing of (?) his …], his valor I will praise.
(9) [Marduk (?) … the] merciful one whose turning is near,
(10) [My request (?)] he considered, he established friendship.
(11) His heart [grew calm], he became merciful.
(12) [He heard] my prayer, he turned his neck.

(13) [His heart] grew calm, he became friendly.
(14) [The Elami]te who did not reverence his great divinity.
(15) [Against] his exalted divinity they spoke blasphemy.
(16) [ ] your weapon to the haughty Elamite.
(17) [You dispersed] his army, you scattered his host.
(18) [His] numerous [people] you quenched like glowing coals.
(19) [His] great […] you flattened like a flood.
(20) [His inhabited places] you laid waste, you left his land fallow.
(21) [His cities] you flattened, into tells you turned (them).

Rev.

(1) [ ] the gods which were inquired of (?)
(2) [ ] like a jug you smashed.
(3) [ ] the temple was devastated.
(4) [ ] the offerings were cut off.
(5) [ ] his protective deity he led away (?).
(6) [ ] his [favorable genie] was scattered.
(7) [ ] was given to the fire god to devour.
(8) [ ] like a jug you smashed.
(9) [ ] his reign you overthrew.
(10) [ ] he became haughty in himself.
(11) [ ] he trusted in (his own) strength.
(12) [ ] he did not remember your divinity.
(13) [ ] your weapons overtook him.
(14) [ ] destroyed the enemy country.
(15) [ ] in joy you scattered.
(16) [you dest]royed his offspring.
(17) [ ] his reign you overthrew.
(18) [ ] you destroyed the enemy.
(19) [ ] your honored name.
(20) [ ] who did not keep his oath.
(21) [ ] you quenched like glowing coals.
(22) [ ] his might
(23) [ ] his name
(24) [ ] fearsome
(25) [ ] help
(26) [ ] my enemies
(27) [ ] his name

(traces)

Text 5: Knudtzon 149

(1) [Šamaš (^{d}UTU) bēlu(EN) rabû(GAL-ú) šá a-šal-lu-ka an-n]a kīna(GI.NA) ⸢a⸣[-pùl-an-ni]

(2) [Šamaš-šum-ukīn (^{md}GIŠ.ŠIR-MU-GI.NA) mār(DUMU) Aššur-aḫ-idd]ina ([^{md}Aššur ŠEŠ-SÙ]M-na) šar(LUGAL) mā[t](KU[R]) [Aššur^{ki}]

(3) [i-na libbi(ŠÀ) šatti(MU.AN.NA) annīti (BÍ-ti) qa?-a]t? bēli(EN) rabî(GAL-i) ^{d}[Marduk(AMAR.UTU)]

(4) [i-n]a lìb-bi āli(URU^{ki}) li-iṣ-bat-ma {a na} i-na pa-a[n Bēl(^{d}EN)]

(5) a-na Babili(KÁ.DINGIR.RA^{ki}) lil-lik eli(UGU) ilūtīka(DINGIR-ti-ka) [rabīt.i(GA.L-ti)]

(6) ù eli(UGU) Bèl(^{d}EN) rabî(GAL-i) Marduk(^{d}AMAR.UTU) ṭab(DÙG.GA[?)]

(7) pa-an ilūtīka(DINGIR-ti-ka) rabīti(GAL-ti) ù pa-an Bèl(^{d}EN) rabî(GAL-i)

(8) Marduk(^{d}AMAR.UTU) ma-ḫi-i ri-il ilūtka(DINGIR-ut-ka) rabīti (GAL-ti) tidê(ZU-e)

(9) [i-na s]alimtim([S]ILIM-tim) i-na pī(KA) ilūtīka(DINGIR-ti-ka) rabīti(GAL-ti) Šamaš(^{d}UTU) bēlu(EN) rabû(GAL-u)

(10) [qa-bi-]i ku-un āmira(IGI-ra) immar(IGI-mar) še-mu-ú išemmê(ŠE-e)

(11) [e-zib šá di-in u$_4$-m]e annî(BÍ-i) kima(GIM) ṭab(DÙG.GA) kima (GIM) ḫa-ṭu-ú ūmu(UD) erpu(ŠÚ-pu) zu-nu(ŠÈG) izannun(ŠUR)

(12) [e-zib šá ellu(KÙ) lu-'-]ú niqi(SIZKUR$_x$) ilputu(TAG-tú) lu-ú a-na pan(IGI) niqi(SIZKUR$_x$) ipriku(GIL.MEŠ)

(13) [e-zibšá lu-]'-ú-tu ašar(KI) bīri(MÁŠ) usanniquma(DIB.DIB-ma) ú-l[e-]'-ú

Rev.

(1) [e-zib šá immer(UDU.NITÀ)] ilūtīka(DINGIR-ti-ka) šá a-na bīri (MÁŠ) ibū(MÁŠ-ú) maṭū(LÁ-ú) ḫa-ṭu-[ú]

(2) [e-zib šá lāp]it([TA]G-it) pūt(SAG.KI) immeri(UDU.NITÀ) ṣubat (TÚG) gi-ni-e-šá ar-šat lab-šú [mim-ma] lu-'-ú

(3) [ikulu(KÚ)] ištû(NAG) ipšušu(ŠEŠ-šú) ku-un qat(ŠU) enû(BAL-ú) uš-pi-lu$_4$

(4) e-zib šá a-na-ku mār(DUMU) bāri(^{lú}ḪAL) ardīka(ÌR-ka) ṣubat(TÚG) gi-ni-e-a lab-šá-ku ú-lu ta-mit

(5) i-na pīya(KA-ya) up-tar-ri-du lu-ú nasḫā(ZI.MEŠ) lu-ú bêrā(BAR.MEŠ)
(6) a-šal-ka Šamaš(^{d}UTU) bēlu(EN) rabû(GAL-ú) ki-i Šamaš-šum-ukin (^{md}GIŠ.ŠIR-MU-GI.NA)
(7) mār(DUMU) Aššur-aḫ-iddina(^{md}Aššur-ŠEŠ-SUM-na) šar(LUGAL) māt(KUR) Aššur^{ki} i-na libbi(ŠÀ) šatti(MU.AN.NA) annīti(BÍ-ti)
(8) qa-at bēli(EN) rabî(GAL-i) Marduk(^{d}[AMAR].U[TU) i]-na libbi(ŠÀ) āli(URU) i-sab-bat-ú-ma
(9) i-na pa-an Bēl(^{d}EN) illaku(GIN-ku)[-ma eli(UG]U) Bēl(^{d}EN) rabî (GAL-i) Marduk^{d}AMAR.UTU) ṭāb(DÙG.GA)
(10) pa?-an? bēl(EN) rabî(GAL-i) Marduk(^{d}AMAR.UTU) maḫ-ru i-na libbi(ŠÀ) immeri(UDU.NITÀ) annî(BÍ-i)
(11) [šuzzizz]amma([Gub-za]-am-ma) an-na kīna(GI.NA) uṣurāti(GIŠ.ḪUR.MEŠ) šalmāti (SILIM.MEŠ) šīrī (UZU.MEŠ) ta-mit
(12) [damqāti(SIG$_5$.M]EŠ) šalmāti (SILIM.MEŠ) šá salimtim(SILIM-tim) šá pi(KA) ilūtīka(DINGIR-ti-ka) rabīti(GAL-ti)
(13) [šuk]-nam-ma lu-m[ur]
(14) [eli(UGU) ilūt]īka([DINGIR-t]i-ka) rabīti(GAL-ti) Šamaš(^{d}UTU) bēlu(EN) rabû(GAL-u) lil-lik-m[a tērtu(KIN) ti-tap-pal]
(15) [? Nisan]nu([? ^{itu}BARA]G) UD-23-KAM lim-me ^{m}Ma-ri-la-rim ina(AŠ) bīt(E)-[ridūti(UŠ)]
(1) O Samas, great lord, what I ask you answer me with a firm yes:
(2) "Shall Samas-sum-ukin the son of Esarhaddon, king of Assyria,
(3) take the hand of the great lord Marduk this year
(4) in the city (Assur) and go before Bel
(5) to Babylon? Would it be pleasing to your great divinity
(6) and to the great lord Marduk?
(7) Would it be acceptable before your great divinity and before
(8) the great lord Marduk? Your great divinity knows.
(9) In a favorable case by the command of your great divinity, O Samas great lord,
(10) will it be commanded, will it be established so that the seer can see and the hearer can hear?"
(11) Disregard it whether this day is good or bad, cloudy or rainy.
(12) Disregard it if a clean or unclean man has touched the sacrifice or has walked in front of the sacrifice.
(13) Disregard it if an unclean woman has approached the place of divination so as to defile it.

(1) Disregard it if the sheep for your divinity upon which they did the extispicy was lacking or deficient.
(2) Disregard it if the one offering the sheep was dressed in soiled everyday clothes or if anything unclean
(3) he has eaten, drunk, or used for anointing, or if he has changed or mixed up the procedure.
(4) Disregard it if I the diviner, your servant, was dressed in my everyday clothes or if the (words) of the request for the oracle
(5) were confused in my mouth, or some were left out, or only a selection were recited.
(6) I ask you O Samas, great lord, whether Samas-sum-ukin
(7) son of Esarhaddon, king of Assyria, should take the hand of the
(8) great lord Marduk this year in the city (Assur)
(9) and go before Bel? Would it be pleasing to the great lord Marduk?
(10) Would it be acceptable before the great lord Marduk? Place
(11) (the answer) inside this sheep and give a firm yes by wholesome markings and favorable, wholesome oracle flesh
(12) indicating the favorable utterance of your great divinity so
(13) that I may see it.
(14) Let it come before your great divinity O Samas, great lord, and answer the extispicy.
(15) The 23rd day of Nisan in the limmu-ship of Marilarim in the Bit-reduti.

Text 6: Knudtzon 104 and 105

Knudtzon 104 and 105 contain a similar query to text 5 (Knudtzon 149), but both 104 and 105 are badly broken, with the result that the question addressed to Samas in these two texts can be restored only by a close comparison. The following reconstruction is of the second phrasing of the question in the oracle request, but it takes into account the wording of the first phrasing. See 104 obv. 2–4, rev. 6–8; 105 rev. 7–9, and compare Landsberger's translation in *Brief des Bischofs*, 23.

[ki Aššur-aḫ-iddina šar māt Aššur ina libbi] šatti ēribti [bēlu rabû Marduk ina] ^{āl}Aššur ana libbi GIŠ.MÁ.U_5 ušelûma [ana] Bibili illakuma....

Shall [Esarhaddon, king of Assyria, during] this next year have [the great lord Marduk] board a passenger ship in Assur and go to Babylon?

SELECTED BIBLIOGRAPHY

Ackroyd, Peter R. *The First Book of Samuel.* Cambridge: Cambridge University Press, 1971.

Arnold, William R. *Ephod and Ark: A Study in the Records and Religion of the Ancient Hebrews.* Harvard Theological Studies 3. Cambridge: Harvard University Press, 1917.

Bentzen, Aage. "The Cultic Use of the Story of the Ark in Samuel." *JBL 67* (1948): 37–53.

Bernhardt, Karl-Heinz, *Gott und Bild: Ein Beitrag zur Begründung und Deutung des Bilderverbotes im Alten Testament.* Berlin: Evangelische Verlagsanstalt, 1956.

Boer, P. A. H. de. *Research into the Text of I Samuel I–XVI.* Amsterdam: H. J. Paris, 1938.

Borger, Rykle. "Gott Marduk und Gott-König Sulgi als Propheten, Zwei prophetische Texte." *Bibliotheca Orientalis* 28 (1971): 3–24.

———. *Die Inschriften Asarhaddons, Königs von Assyrien.* AfO Beiheft 9. Graz: Weidner, 1956.

———. *Handbuch der Keilschriftliteratur.* 3 vols. Berlin: de Gruyter, 1967–1975.

Bourke, Joseph. "Samuel and the Ark: A Study in Contrasts." *Dominican Studies* 7 (1954): 73–103.

Brinkman, John A. *A Political History of Post-Kassite Babylonia 1158–722 B.C.* Analecta Orientalia 43. Rome: Pontifical Biblical Institute, 1968.

———. "A Preliminary Catalogue of Written Sources for a Political History of Babylonia: 1160–722 B.C." *JCS* 16 (1962): 83–109.

Budde, Karl. *Die Bücher Samuel.* KHC 8. Tübingen: Mohr Siebeck, 1902.

Campbell, Antony. *The Ark Narrative (1 Sam 4–6; 2 Sam 6): A Form-Critical and Traditio-Historical Study.* SBLDS 16. Missoula, Mont.: SBL and Scholars' Press, 1975.

Caspari, Wilhelm. *Die Samuelbücher.* KAT 7. Leipzig: Deichertsche Verlagsbuchhandlung, 1926.

Cassuto, U. *The Goddess Anath.* Translated by I. Abrahams. Jerusalem: Magnes, 1971.

Childs, B. S. "A Study of the Formula 'Until This Day!'" *JBL* 82 (1963): 279–92.

———. *The Book of Exodus.* OTL. Philadelphia: Westminster, 1974.

Clerc, Charly. "Les théories relatives au culte des images chez les auteurs grecs du IIme siècle après J.-C." Doctoral Thesis. University of Paris. Paris, 1915.

Coats, G. W. "Despoiling the Egyptians." *VT* 18 (1968): 450–57.

Cogan, Morton. *Imperialism and Religion: Assyria, Judah and Israel in the Eighth and Seventh Centuries B.C.E.* SBLMS 19. Missoula, Mont.: SBL and Scholars Press, 1974.

Cross, F. M. *Canaanite Myth and Hebrew Epic: Essays in the History of the Religion of Israel.* Cambridge: Harvard University Press, 1973.

Dahood, M. J. "Hebrew-Ugaritic Lexicography II." *Biblica* 45 (1964): 393–412.

———. *Ras Shamra Parallels.* Vol. 1. Rome: Pontifical Biblical Institute, 1972.

———. *Ugaritic-Hebrew Philology.* Rome: Pontifical Biblical Institute, 1965.

Delcor, M. "Jahweh et Dagon ou le Jahwisme face à la religion des Philistins, d'après 1 Sam. V." *VT* 14 (1964): 136–54.

Dhorme, Paul. *Les livres de Samuel.* Études Bibliques. Paris: Gabalda, 1910.

Donner, Herbert. "Die Schwellenhüpfer: Beobachtungen zu Zephanja 1, 8F." *JSS* 15 (1970): 42–55.

Driver, G. R. "The Plague of the Philistines (1 Samuel v, 6–vi, 16)." *JRAS* (1950): 50–51.

Driver, S. R. *Notes on the Hebrew Text of the Books of Samuel.* Oxford: Clarendon, 1890.

Dus, J. "Die Erzählung über den Verlust der Lade, 1 Sam. IV." *VT* 13 (1963): 333–37.

Edzard, O. "Mesopotamien." *Wörterbuch der Mythologie.* Edited by H. W. Haussig. Vol. 1. Stuttgart: Ernst Klett, 1965.

Ehrlich, Arnold B. *Randglossen zur hebraischen Bibel* III. Leipzig: Hinrichs, 1910.

Eising, H. "Der Weisheitslehrer und die Götterbilder." *Biblica* 40 (1959): 393–408.

Fraine, J. de. "La royauté de Yahvé dans les textes concernant l'arche." *SVT* 15 (1966): 134–49.

Geffcken, Johannes. "Der Bilderstreit des heidnischen Altertums." *Archiv für Religionswissenschaft* 19 (1916–19): 286–315.

Grayson, A. K. "Chronicles and the Akitu Festival." *Actes de la XVIIe Rencontre Assyriologique Internationale* (Brussels, 1970): 160–70.

Gressmann, Hugo. *Altorientalische Texte zum Alten Testament.* Berlin: de Gruyter, 1926.

———. *Die alteste Geschichtsschreibung und Prophetie Israels.* SAT 2/1. Göttingen: Vandenhoeck & Ruprecht, 1921.

Hertzberg, Hans Wilhelm. *Die Samuelbücher.* ATD 10. Göttingen: Vandenhoeck & Ruprecht, 1968.

Hölscher, Gustav, *Die Anfänge der hebraischen Geschichtsschreibung.* Sitzungsberichte der Heidelberger Akademie der Wissenschaften, Philosophisch-historische Klasse, 1941/42, 3. Heidelberg: Winter, 1942.

Hylander, Ivar. *Der literarische Samuel-Saul-Komplex (1 Sam. 1–15) traditionsgeschichtlich untersucht.* Uppsala: Almqvist & Wiksell, 1932.

Jackson, J. J. "The Ark Narratives: An Historical, Textual, and Form-Critical Study of I Samuel 4–6 and II Samuel 6." Union Theological Seminary Dissertation, 1962.

Jacobsen, Thorkild. "Religious Drama in Ancient Mesopotamia." In *Unity and Diversity: Essays in the History, Literature, and Religion of the Ancient Near East.* Edited by H. Goedicke and J. J. M. Roberts. Baltimore: Johns Hopkins University Press, 1975.

King, L. W. *Chronicles Concerning Early Babylonian Kings.* 2 vols. London: Luzac, 1907.

Knudtzon, J. A. *Assyrische Gebete an den Sonnengott für Staat und königliches Haus aus der Zeit Asarhaddons und Asurbanipals.* 2 vols. Leipzig: Pfeiffer, 1893.

Kosters, W. H. "De verhalen over de ark in Samuel." *Theologische Tijdschrift* (1893): 361–78.

Kristensen, *De Ark van Jahwe.* Mededeelingen der koninklijke Akademie van Wetenschappen, Afdeeling Litterkunde Deel 76, B/5. Amsterdam: N. V. Noord-Hollandsche Uitgevers-Maatschappij, 1933.

Lambert, W. G. "Emmeduranki and Related Matters." *JCS* 21 (1967): 126–38.

———. "Three Unpublished Fragments of the Tukulti-Ninurta Epic." *AfO* 18 (1957): 38–51.

Lambert, W. G., and A. R. Millard. *Atra-hasīs: The Babylonian Story of the Flood.* Oxford: Clarendon, 1969.

Landsberger, Benno. *Brief des Bischofs von Esagila an König Asarhaddon.* Medelingen der Koninklijke Nederlandse Akademie van Wetsenschappen, AFD. Letterkunde, Nieuwe Reeks 28/6. Amsterdam, 1965.

Langdon, Stephen. *Die neubabylonischen Königsinschriften.* VAB 4. Leipzig: Hinrichs, 1912.

Lie, A. G. *The Inscriptions of Sargon II, King of Assyria.* 2 vols. Paris: Geuthner, 1929.

Luckenbill, D. D. *Ancient Records of Assyria and Babylonia.* 2 vols. Chicago: University of Chicago Press, 1926.

———. *The Annals of Sennacherib.* Chicago: University of Chicago Press, 1924.

Maier, Johann. *Das altisraelitische Ladeheiligtum.* BZAW 93. Töpelmann, 1965.

Miller, P. D., Jr. *The Divine Warrior in Early Israel.* Cambridge: Harvard University Press, 1973. Repr., Atlanta: Society of Biblical Literature, 2006.

Montalbano, F. J. "Canaanite Dagon: Origin, Nature." *CBQ* 13 (1951): 381–97.

Moran, W. L. "The End of the Unholy War and the Anti-Exodus." *Biblica* 44 (1963): 333–42.

Mowinckel, Sigmund. *Psalmenstudien II.* Videnskapsselskapets Skrifter, 2. Hist.-Filos, Klasse 1921/6. Kristiania: Dybwad, 1922.

———. *The Psalms in Israel's Worship.* 2 vols. New York: Abingdon, 1962.

Nielsen, Eduard. "The Burial of the Foreign Gods." *Studia Theologica* 7–8 (1953–54): 103–22.

———. "Some Reflections on the History of the Ark." *SVT* 7 (1959): 61–74.

Noth, M. *Überlieferungsgeschichtliche Studien I: Die Sammelnden und bearbeitenden Geschichtswerke im Alten Testament.* Darmstadt: Wissenschaftliche Buchgesellschaft, 1963. (A photo-offset reproduction of the first edition, Halle an der Saale, 1943 = Schriften der Königsberger Gelehrten Gesellschaft. Geisteswissenschaftliche Klasse, 18, 1943, pp. 43–266).

Nowack, W. *Richter, Ruth u. Bücher Samuelis.* HAT 1/4. Göttingen: Vandenhoeck & Ruprecht, 1902.

Peters, Norbert. *Beitrage zur Text- und Literarkritik sowie zur Erklarung der Bücher Samuel.* Freiburg im Breisgau: Herder, 1899.

Pope, Marvin, and Röllig, Wolfgang. "Die Mythologie der Ugariter und Phönizier." *Wörterbuch der Mythologie* I. Edited by H. W. Haussig. Stuttgart: Klett, 1962.

Porter, J. R. "The Interpretation of 2 Samuel VI and Psalm CXXXII." *JTS* NS 5 (1954): 161–73.

Postgate, J. N. *The Governor's Palace Archive.* Texts from Nimrud II. British School of Archaeology in Iraq, 1973.

———. "Two Marduk Ordeal Fragments." *ZA* NF 60 (1970): 124–27.

Press, R. "Der Prophet Samuel: Eine traditions-geschichtliche Untersuchung." *ZAW* 56 (1938): 177–225.

Preuss, H. D. *Verspottung fremder Religionen im Alten Testament.* BWANT 12. Stuttgart: Kohlhammer, 1971.

Roberts, J. J. M. "The Hand of Yahweh." *VT* 21 (1971): 244–51.

Rost, Leonhard. *Die Überlieferung von der Thronnachfolge Davids.* BWANT 111/6. Stuttgart: Kohlhammer, 1926. Reprinted in Rost's *Das Kleine Credo und andere Studien zum Alten Testament* (Heidelberg: Quelle & Meyer, 1965), 119–253.

Rost, Paul. *Die Keilschrifttexte Tiglat-Pilesers III.* 2 vols. Leipzig: Pfeiffer, 1893.

Schicklberger, Franz. *Die Ladeerzählungen des ersten Samuel-Buches, Eine literaturwissenschaftliche und theologiegeschichtliche Untersuchung.* Forschung zur Bibel 7. Würzburg: Echter, 1973.

Schlögl, P. Nivard. *Die Bücher Samuels.* Kurzgefasster Wissenschaftlicher Commentar zu den Heiligen Schriften des Alten Testaments 1/3/1. Vienna: Mayer, 1904.

Schott, A. "Die Anfänge Marduks als eines assyrischen Gottes." *ZA* NF 9 (1936): 318–21.

Schulz, Alfons. *Die Bücher Samuel.* EHAT 8. Münster: Aschendorff, 1919.

Schunck, Klaus-Dietrich. *Benjamin: Untersuchungen zur Enstehung und Geschichte eines israelitischen Stammes.* BZAW 86. Berlin: Töpelmann, 1963.

Smith, Henry Preserved. *The Books of Samuel.* ICC. Edinburgh: T&T Clark, 1899.

Smith, Sidney. *Babylonian Historical Texts Relating to the Capture and Downfall of Babylon.* London: Methuen, 1924.

Soden, W. von. "Gibt es ein Zeugnis dass die Babylonier an Marduks Wiederauferstehung glaubten?" *ZA* NF 17 (1955): 130–66.

———. "Ein neues Bruckstück des assyrischen Kommentars zum Marduk-Ordal." *ZA* NF 18 (1957): 224–34.

Spycket, Agnès. *Les statues de culte dans les textes mesopotamiens des origines à la Ire dynastie de Babylone.* Cahiers de la Revue Biblique. Paris: Gabalda, 1968.

Stoebe, Hans Joachim. *Das erste Buch Samuelis.* KAT 8/1. Gütersloh: Mohn, 1973.

Streck, M. *Assurbanipal und die letzten assyrischen Könige bis zum Untergange Niniveh's.* 3 vols. VAB 7. Leipzig: Hinrichs, 1916.

Sturtevant, E. H., and G. Bechtel. *A Hittite Chrestomathy.* Philadelphia: Linguistic Society of America, 1935.

Thenius, Otto. *Die Bücher Samuels.* KeH 4. Leipzig: Hirzel, 1864.

Thiersch, Hermann. *Ependytes und Ephod: Gottesbild und Priesterkleid im Alten Vorderasien.* Geisteswissenschaftlichen Forschungen 8. Stuttgart: Kohlhammer, 1936.

Thomas, Winton. "A Note on וְנוֹדַע לָכֶם in I Samuel VI,3." *JTS* 11 (1960): 52.

Tur-Sinai, N. H. "The Ark of God at Beit Shemesh (I Sam. VI) and Peres 'Uzza (2 Sam. VI; 1 Chron. XIII)." *VT* 1 (1951): 275–86.

Vaux, R. de. *Les livres de Samuel.* La Sainte Bible. Paris: Cerf, 1961.

Virolleaud, C. *La déese 'Anat.* Mission de Ras Shamra 4. Paris: Geuthner, 1938.

Vriezen, Th. C. "De Compositie van de Samuël-Boeken." *Orientalia Neerlandica.* Oostersch Genootschap in Nederland. Leiden: Sijthoff, 1948, 167–86; "Résumé," 187–89.

Wanke, G. "*'ôy* and *hôy.*" *ZAW* 78 (1966): 215–18.

Weidner, E. "Studien zur Zeitgeschichte Tukulti-Ninurtas I." *AfO* 13 (1939/40): 109–24.

Weippert, Manfred. "'Heiliger Krieg' in Israel und Assyrien." *ZAW* 84 (1972): 460–93.

Weiser, Artur. *The Old Testament: Its Formation and Development.* Translated by Dorothea M. Barton. New York: Association Press, 1961.

Wellhausen, Julius. *Der Text der Bücher Samuelis.* Göttingen: Vandenhoeck & Ruprecht, 1871.

Willis, John. "An Anti-Elide Narrative Tradition from a Prophetic Circle at the Ramah Sanctuary." *JBL* 90 (1971): 288–308.

INDEX OF BIBLICAL AND RELATED CITATIONS

Genesis
17:3 59
50:15 65

Exodus
3:20–21 73
3:22 73
9:3 63, 66
10:1–2 73
10:2 73
12:36 73
28:3 36
28:41 36
29:1 36
29:44 36
30:30 36
40:13 36

Leviticus
7:31ff. 38
8:30 36
21:8 36

Numbers
1:53 36, 78
3:10 36, 78
3:31 36
18:3 36
19:2 73
31:30 36
31:47 36
35:9–28 40

Deuteronomy
18:3 38
21:3–4 73
21:8 70

Joshua
5:14 59
6:5 45
7:1–9 27
7:6 59
10:25 47

Judges
2:10 37
5:23 60
6:26 7
7:20 45
10:17 44
11:1–3 29
11:4–28 29
11:29–33 29
13:2–25 29
14:1–18 29
14:19–20 29
15:1–6 29
15:7–18 29
15:9–13 29
15:14–20 29
16 55
16:1–27 29
16:28–31 29
20:19–21 44

1 Samuel
1–3 28, 30, 31, 32, 50, 88
1–4 29
1–7 27, 28, 29

1 Samuel (*cont.*)
1:1–4:1a 29
1:3 37
2 31, 41, 80, 82, 83, 84, 88
2:12 37, 38, 81
2:12–17 28, 30, 31, 32, 35, **37–39**, 50, 80, **81**, 82
2:12ff. 89, 92
2:13 38
2:13–14 38
2:14 38
2:15 38
2:16 39, 41
2:17 39, 81
2:22 39
2:22–25 28, 30, 31, 32, 35, **39–40**, 50, 80, **81**, 82
2:23 39
2:25 40, 47, 81, 89
2:25a 39
2:25b 40
2:27 40
2:27–36 30, 31, 32, 35, **40–41**, 50, 80, **82**
2:27ff. 89
2:28 40
2:29a 40
2:30–31 41
2:30ff. 89
2:31 41
2:32 41
2:33 41
2:34 41, 47, 49
2:35 41
3 30
3:7 37
3:12 30
3:21 28
4 2, 3, 6, 9, 29, 31, 32, 35, **43–52**, 53, 56, **82–85**, 86, 88, 89
4–6 31, 32, 33, 37, 50, 53, 55, 88, 92
4–7 34
4–7:1 34
4:1 2, 3, 5
4:1a 43
4:1b 27
4:1–4 **43–44**, 45
4:1b–4 80, 82, 84
4:1b–7 29
4:1b–9 88
4:1b–11 **43–47**, 80, **82–84**
4:1b–22 80
4:1b–7:1 9, 27, 28, 29, 30, 31, 32, 35, 78
4:2 43
4:2–4 2, 3, 5
4:3 10, 45, 53, 54
4:3–4 44
4:4 3, 28, 44, 47, 54
4:5 3, 44, 54, 62
4:5–9 3, 5, 6, 45, 48, 53, 54, 89
4:5–11 **44–47**, 80, 83, 84
4:6 48, 54, 84
4:7 45, 56, 65
4:8 63, 64, 74, 87, 90
4:9 3, 5, 47, 53
4:10 3, 45, 47, 48
4:10–11 88
4:10–12 2, 3, 5
4:10–22 53, 54
4:11 54, 56, 84
4:11–18 52
4:12–18 **48–51**, 80
4:12–22 **48–52**, 80, **84–85**
4:13 2, 3, 5, 28, 48, 49, 54
4:13a 48
4:13b 48
4:14 48
4:14a 48
4:14b–18a 2, 3, 5
4:15ff. 81
4:16 48
4:17 49, 50, 54, 56
4:17–18 82
4:18 30, 49, 50, 51, 54

4:19 50, 51, 54, 56
4:19–21 2, 3, 5, 52
4:19–22 48, **51–52**, 80
4:20 52
4:21 5, 51, 54, 56
4:22 9, 51, 54, 56
5 45, 51, **53–67**, 69, 74, 83, 84, **85–86**, 90
5–6 2, 3, 47
5:1 54, 55, 90
5:1a 53
5:1–2 88
5:1–4 61
5:1–5 13, 53, **54–61**, 65, 72, 80, 86, 89
5:1–6bα 6
5:1–12 80
5:1–7:1 29, **85–88**, 80, 85
5:2 54, 55
5:2a 54
5:2–4(5) 54
5:2–5 54, 55
5:3 54, 55, 58, 59, 60
5:3–5 88
5:4 54, 55, 58, 60, 61, 64, 90
5:4b 55
5:5 61, 93
5:6 47, 54, 62, 63, 64
5:6–12 53, **61–67**, 80, 86
5:7 54, 63, 64, 65, 66
5:7–12 6
5:8 54, 66, 67
5:9 11, 47, 63, 64, 66
5:10 54, 62, 67
5:11 54, 63, 64
5:12 47, 57
5:19 53
5:21 53
5:22 53
6 53, 54, **69–78**, 83, 85, 86
6:1 54, 62, 69, 86
6:1–4 6
6:1–9 **69–74**, 80, 86
6:1–7:1 80, **86–88**
6:2 54, 69
6:3 54, 64, 71, 86
6:3ff. 69
6:4 47, 76
6:4ff. 71
6:5 63, 64, 71, 72, 76, 86
6:5–9 9, 74
6:5aβ–11abα 6
6:6 72, 73, 74
6:7–9 73
6:7ff. 69
6:8 54, 73
6:9 63, 64, 74, 75, 86
6:10 74
6:10–16 **75**, 80, 86
6:11 54
6:12 75
6:12–14 6
6:13 75
6:14 7
6:15 54, 75
6:16 6, 75, 86
6:17 62, 66
6:17–18a 75, 76
6:17–18 9, 72, **75–76**, 80, 87
6:18 54, 71, 76
6:18b 76
6:19 54
6:19–7:1 **77–78**, 80
6:19b 77
6:20 77, 87
6:21 34, 54, 77
6:30 63
7 32, 41
7:1 30, 33, 34, 35, 36, 54, 77
7:2 29
7:2–17 29, 32
8:1–3 37
8:5 39
9–10 29
11:1–4 29
11:5–11 29

1 Samuel (*cont.*)
14:49 35
16 29
17:1–30 29
17:20 45
17:31–54 29
17:49 59
17:52 45
18:17ff. 35
19:11ff. 35
21 35
23 35
25:44 35
28:16–19 32
31 32

2 Samuel 89
1:4 49
2:17 43
2:35 36
3:12ff. 35
5:17–21 92
5:21 93
6 1, 2, 6, 9, 24, 25, 32, 33, 34, 35, 77, 92, 107
6:1 24, 33
6:2 34
6:2–23 9
6:5 24
6:13 25
6:14–15 24
6:16 9, 35
6:20–23 9, 35
8:17 35
10:12 47
10:15–18 44
11:27 40
12:7ff. 89
12:24 40
15:24 35
17:14 40
18:6–8 44
21:8 35

1 Kings 89
2:26–27 35
2:27 30, 36
2:35 35
4:4 35
8:22 16
8:25 16
18 7
20:26–30 44

2 Kings
18:30–35 15

1 Chronicles
13:5 33

2 Chronicles
20:21–22 45
25:14 57

Job
9:2 65

Psalms
74 61
89 61
106:30 40

Isaiah
27 61
41:21–29 18
44:6–8 18
45:20–21 18
48:3–8 18
51 61
51:5–7 18
51:9ff. 60

Jeremiah
21:5–6 64
44:15–19 18

Ezekiel
3:23 59
10–11 56
16:52 40
43:3 59
44:4 59

Hosea
10:5 56

Habakkuk
3:5 64

Zephaniah
1:9 9

Zechariah
14:13 65

Syriac Apocalypse of Baruch
4:2–7 25
5:3 25
6:1–10 25
7:1–8:2 25

Baruch
6:15 25
6:48–49 25
6:56–58 25

Epistle of Jeremiah
1:15 25
1:48–49 25
1:56–58 25

INDEX OF AUTHORS

Arnold, William R. 25
Bechtel, G. 16
Bentzen, Aage 2, 55
Borger, Rykle viii, 14, 16, 17, 21, 95
Campbell, Antony 1, 2, 9, 10, 11, 12, 13, 27, 31, 32, 33, 37, 54, 55, 58, 69, 72, 75, 76, 79, 92
Cassuto, Umberto 60
Childs, Brevard S. 61, 73
Coats, George W. 73
Cogan, Morton 13, 15, 21, 56, 57
Cross, Frank Moore 36, 39, 40, 43, 45, 46, 55, 62, 70, 77
Dahood, Mitchell J. 8, 46
Delcor, M. 1, 2, 12, 55, 58
Donner, Herbert 9
Driver, S. R. 43, 45, 46, 55, 58, 62, 75, 76, 77
Dus, J. 31
Edzard, O 21
Ehrlich, Arnold 62, 65
Eissfeldt, Otto viii
Goetze, Albrecht 70, 72
Grayson, A. K. 20
Hertzberg, Hans Wilhelm 25
Hölscher, Gustav 24
Jackson, J. J. 43
Jacobsen, Thorkild 21
King, L. W. 16
Knudtzon, J. A. 8, 22, 103, 105
Kosters, W. H. 24
Lambert, W. G. 15, 19, 72
Landsberger, Benno 16, 20, 105
Langdon, Stephen 23
Lie, A. G. 14, 15
Luckenbill, D. D. 14, 16, 21, 56
Millard, A. R. 72
Miller, P. D., Jr. 45, 58, 60
Montalbano, F. J. 55
Moran, W. L. 47
Mowinckel, Sigmund 2, 24
Noth, Martin 40, 41
Pope, Marvin 60, 61
Postgate. J. N. 21
Press, R. 28
Preuss, H. D. 13
Roberts, J. J. M. 8, 21, 63
Rost, Leonhard 1, 2, 3, 9, 27, 28, 32, 33, 51, 74, 79, 89
Rost, Paul 15
Schicklberger, Franz 1, 2, 3, 4, 5, 6, 7, 8, 9, 12, 13, 31, 32, 33, 34, 43, 44, 48, 49, 50, 51, 52, 53, 54, 55, 62, 72, 75, 76, 77, 79
Schott, A. 21
Schulz, Alfons 41
Schunck, Klaus-Dietrich 33, 92
Smith, H. P. 28, 38, 40, 43, 45, 46, 48
Smith, Sidney 13
Soden, W. von 21
Spycket, Agnès 13
Stoebe, Hans Joachim 2, 41, 55, 62, 72, 73, 75
Streck, M. 14, 15, 22
Sturtevant, E. H. 16
Thenius, Otto 70
Thomas, Winton 70
Vaux, Roland de 25

Virolleaud, C. 60
Vriezen, Th. C. 34, 92
Wanke, G. 46
Weidner, E. 14, 16, 21
Weiher, E. von 8
Weippert, Manfred 20
Wellhausen, Julius 45, 46, 48, 51, 55, 58, 76
Willis, John 27, 28, 29, 30, 32, 35, 62, 75, 78

CPSIA information can be obtained at www.ICGtesting.com
262938BV00002B/18/P

9 781589 832947